ÖDÖN VON HORVÁTH: PLAYS TWO

Ödön von Horváth

PLAYS TWO

ITALIAN NIGHT
translated by Meredith Oakes

TALES FROM THE VIENNA WOODS
translated by Christopher Hampton

OBERON BOOKS
LONDON
WWW.OBERONBOOKS.COM

Contents

CHRONOLOGY

Titles have been given literal translations, unless there is a more famous alternative in English.

1901 9 December: Ödön (Edmund) Josef von Horváth born in Susak, a suburb of Fiume. Father: Dr. Ödön Josef von Horváth, diplomat. Mother: Maria Hermine, née Prehnal.

1902 Summer: family moves to Belgrade.

1903 6 July: brother Lajos von Horváth is born in Belgrade.

1908 Family moves to Budapest. First classes taught in Hungarian at home.

1909 Dr Horváth is called to Munich. Ödön stays in Budapest where he attends the *Rákóczianum* (archbishopal boarding school), and receives an intensive religious education.

1913 December: Ödön joins his parents in Munich.

1914 Ödön attends the *Wilhelmsgymnasium* in Munich. First differences with the religious education teacher Dr Heinzinger, which remain strong for years and later appear in Ödön's works. Dr Horváth is conscripted into the army.

1915 Dr Horváth is called away from the front back to Munich.

1916 Family moves to Pressburg. First attempts at writing, in the form of poetry, of which one, *Luci in Macbeth*. *Eine Zwerggeschichte* (A Dwarf Story) *von Ed. v. Horváth* survives. Friends of the time also tell of other 'occasional poems' eg *Professoren in der Unterwelt* (Teachers in Hades) etc.

1918 Before the end of the war Dr Horváth is called to Budapest. There Ödön meets a circle of young people (The Galileo Circle), who read the national-revolutionary works of Endre Ady with enthusiasm. Strong interest in the political power games in Budapest.

1919 Spring: Dr Horváth is called to Munich. Ödön is sent to his uncle in Vienna and attends the *Realgymnasium.* Summer: *Abitur* (A-Levels) in Vienna, then moves to Munich.
Autumn: Enrolled at the Ludwig-Maximillian University in Munich (until the winter semester of 1921/22).

1920 Meets Siegfried Kallenberg in Munich, who encourages him to write *Das Buch der Tänze* (The Book of Dances).

1922 *Das Buch der Tänze* published by *El Schahin* of Munich. Later, in 1926, Ödön buys all remaining books with the help of his father and destroys all available copies. 7 February: *Das Buch der Tänze* is shown together with *Buch der Frühen Weisen* (Book of Early Songs) and *Aus dem Herbst* (From Autumn) in the Steinicke-Saal in Munich, for the 'First Literary-Musical Evening of the Kallenberg-Society'. More attempts at writing, probably including *Ein Epilog* and the 'romantic novella' *Amazonas.*

1923 Ödön moves to his parents' country house in Murnau. Intensive period of writing, but he destroys most of his documents. Probably wrote the fragment *Dósa* and the play *Mord in der Mohrengasse* (Murder in Moor Street), incorporating ideas that were to appear in his later plays. As well as short prose texts he wrote *Sportsmärchen* (Sports Fairy Tales) which were published in various magazines and papers (1924 and later).

1924 26 March: on the occasion of the 'Third Literary-Musical Evening of the Kallenberg-Society' Ödön's plays are once again presented to the public, including *Geschichte einer kleinen Liebe* (The Trivial Love Story), *Ständchen* (Serenade)– with the music of Siegfried Kallenberg – and *Schlaf meine kleine Braut* (Sleep, My Little Bride) which has since been lost. In autumn Ödön goes on a Paris trip for a several weeks with his brother Lajos, after which he decides to settle down in Berlin.

1926 20 February: *Das Buch der Tänze* has its premiere at the Stadttheater Osnabruck.
The popular play *Revolte auf Cote 3018* (Revolt on Gradient 3018) and the comedy *Zur schönen Aussicht* (The Belle Vue) were probably written around that time.

1927 In the office of the German League for Human Rights in Berlin, Ödön is sifting through papers for an account of the judicial crisis and finds material about the secret executions of the Black Army. Probably wrote the fragmentary play *Fall Ella Wald* (The Case of Ella Wald) around that time.
4 November: *Revolte auf Cote 3018* premieres in Hamburg. After the premiere, Ödön reworks his play and gives it the title *Die Bergbahn* (The Mountain Railway).

1928 Ödön visits Spain and uses his experiences there in the first part of his novel *Der ewige Spiesser* (The Eternal Philistine). He reworks his history *Sladek oder Die schwarze Armee* (Sladek, or The Black Army) and calls the new version *Sladek der schwarze Reichswehrmann* (Sladek, the Black Soldier).

1929 4 January: *Die Bergbahn* has its première in Berlin. The publishing company Ullstein offers him a contract which allows him to live as an independent writer.

Using an earlier work with the title *Ein Fräulein wird verkauft* (A Young Lady is Sold), Ödön writes the comedy *Rund um den Kongreß* (A Sexual Congress). The first chapter of the novel *Herr Reithofer wird selbstlos* (Mr Reithofer Becomes Unselfish) becomes the base of *Der ewige Spießer*. He also continues working on the stories of Agnes Pollinger, drawing from the concept of a '*Roman einer Kellnerin*' (Novel about a Waitress) with the titles *Ursula* and *Charlotte*. Probably starts on his novel *Der Mittelstand* (The Middle Class) around this time.

13 October: The matinée premiere of *Sladek* provokes strong attacks from the Nazis.

1930 Ödön finishes his novel *Der ewige Spießer* and hands it to the publishers Propyläen, whose drama department Arcadia also publishes his plays.

Several writer evenings, also in Munich.

People and events of his life reappear in his play *Italienische Nacht* (Italian Night).

1931 20 March: *Italenische Nacht* has its première in Berlin.

4 July: Oscar Sima directs a non-political version of the play in Vienna. At the premiere, Ödön explains that after a long period of work, he has just finished *Geschichten aus dem Wiener Wald* (Tales from the Vienna Woods).

22/23 July: Ödön is interviewed as a witness in a lawsuit and comes under strong attack from the Nazis. Autumn: Following Carl Zuckmayer's recommendation, Ödön – together with Erik Reger – is given the Kleist prize.

2 November: The premier of *Geschichten aus dem Wiener Wald* at the Deutsches Theatre in Berlin is an important success.

Max Reinhardt pushes Ödön and R.A. Stemmle to write a magazine *Magazin des Glücks* (Magazine of Happiness), together with Walter Mehring. Several drafts are made but never realised.

Ödön finishes his play *Kasimir und Karoline* the same year.

1932 February: meeting with Lucas Kristl in Munich, who inspires Ödön to write a play based on the personal columns in newspapers; *Glaube Liebe Hoffnung* (Faith, Hope and Charity) is based on a real story and reworked several times. Readings by the author in Munich and an interview in April with the *Bayrischen Rundfunk* (Bavarian Radio) are proof of Ödön's growing popularity.

18 November: Premiere of *Kasimir und Karoline* in Leipzig and a week later – the same production – in Berlin. Ödön begins to feel it necessary to write *Gebrauchsanweisung* (directions for use) for his plays.

1933 Heinz Hilpert is forced by the Nazis to put off Ödön's *Glaube Leibe Hoffnung* which he had agreed to premiere. The same happens for other productions of Ödön's plays in German theatres.

Ödön's parents' house in Murnau is searched by SA troops, causing the Hungarian ambassador to protest. Ödön leaves Germany, going to Salzburg and then Vienna.

Der Unbekannte aus der Seine (The Stranger from the Seine) is written.

In order to keep his Hungarian nationality, Ödön has to travel to Budapest. This inspires his comedy *Hin und her* (Back and Forth).

27 December: Ödön marries the singer Maria Elsner in Vienna. They are divorced the following year.

1934 The planned premiere in Vienna of *Die Unbekannte aus der Seine* does not take place.

Ödön returns to Berlin in order to study National Socialism as research for a new play. His impressions find their way into the draft and the scenes of *Der Lenz ist da!* (Spring Has Come!) The same concerns surface later in his novel *Jugend ohne Gott* (Youth Without God).

In Berlin, Ödön makes contacts in the film industry,
develops various scripts, writes film dialogues and
adapts subjects like *Kean* and *Brüderlein fein!* Records
of this time have been largely lost but there are stories
of works with titles such as *Kuss im Parlament* (A Kiss
in Parliament) and *Pässe nach Deutschland* (Passports
to Germany). Later Ödön distances himself from his
work in film.

Using earlier material, Ödön writes the 'fairytale'
Himmelwärts (Heavenbound), which is taken up by a
Berlin company but cannot be produced in Germany.
Ödön writes various drafts with different content using
the same title, and also a novel (*Ludwig Schlamperl*).
The Nazis start new investigations against him.
18 December: Premiere of *Hin und her* in Zurich.
Ödön makes use of this opportunity to leave Germany
together with the Berlin actress Wera Liessem.

1935 Several plans, drawings and fragments around the
topic 'escape from the present' are written. Together
with his brother Lajos, Ödön plans an illustrated
epistolarian novel with the title *Die Reise ins Paradies*
(Journey to Paradise) as a commission for publishers
Max Pfeffer. Ödön writes the comedy *Mit dem Kopf durch
die Wand* (With the Head Through the Wall) which he
reworks several times until completely abandoning it
after its premiere in Vienna (10 December).

1936 Ödön finishes the play *Der jüngste Tag* (Judgement
Day) and rapidly, working from earlier drafts, he
writes the plays *Figaro läßt sich scheiden* (Figaro Gets
Divorced) and *Don Juan kommt aus dem Krieg* (Don
Juan Comes Back from the War). During this time,
Ödön mainly resides in Vienna and in Henndorf near
Salzburg. When he visits his parents in Possenhofen
in August, he is told that his residence visa has been
withdrawn and that he has to leave Germany within
24 hours.
13 November: *Glaube Liebe Hoffnung* has its premiere
under the title *Liebe, Pflicht und Hoffnung* in Vienna.

1937 Ödön distances himself from nearly all his earlier
plays and decides to write a *Komödie des Menschen*
(Comedy of Mankind). This leads him to write the
comedies *Ein Dorf ohne Männer* (A Village Without
Men) and the 'Komodie des Erdbebens' (Earthquake
Comedy) *Pompeji.* These are the only two plays he is
willing to include in his 'comedy of mankind'.
In Henndorf, Ödön writes the novel *Jugend ohne Gott.*
2 April: Premiere of *Figaro läßt sich scheiden* in Prague.
24 September: Premiere of *Ein Dorf ohne Männer* in
Prague.
In autumn, *Jugend ohne Gott* is published by Allert
de Lange in Amsterdam and becomes an enormous
success; many foreign companies acquire the
translation rights. Ödön starts his next novel
Ein Kind unserer Zeit (A Child of our Times).
5 December: Premiere of *Himmelwärts* as a matinee
show in Vienna.
11 December: Premiere of *Der jüngste Tag* in Mahrisch-
Ostrau.
By the end of the year Ödön finishes *Ein Kind unserer
Zeit* which is published by Allert de Lange.

1938 Severe depressions, dissatisfaction in his artistic life
and financial worries stop Ödön from accomplishing
further plans. He only writes a few pages of an idea
for a novel called *Adieu Europa.*
March: His friends escape Germany: Walter Mehring
to Zurich, Hertha Paula to Paris and Franz Theodor
Csokor to Poland. Ödön leaves Vienna too, accepting
Lajos von Hatvany's invitation to go to Ofen.
April-May: Having visited the actress Lydia Busch
in Teplitz-Schönau, Ödön embarks on a series of
journeys that eventually bring him to Paris on 28
May, where he has been invited for discussions with
Armand Pierhal, the translator of *Jugend ohne Gott* and
Ein Kind unserer Zeit, and Robert Siodmak, who wants
to make a film of *Jugend ohne Gott.*

1 June: Another meeting with Robert Siodmak. Ödön plans to travel to Zurich the next morning. Around 7.30 pm, he is killed by a falling tree, opposite the Marigny Theatre.

7 June: Ödön is buried in St Ouen cemetary, north Paris.

ITALIAN NIGHT
ITALIENISCHE NACHT
(1930)

INTRODUCTION

Meredith Oakes

Germany in the 1930s: how did it feel? How did it happen? Horváth's plays are far more illuminating than history books. The reason why they cast so much light on the large-scale forces of inflation, unemployment and the rise of Nazism is that they show these forces at work within fascinating, believable, contradictory, small-scale communities. Horváth is famous for his historical relevance, but he will go on being famous for the classic richness of his human observation.

Nowhere is he richer than in the small-town plays of which *Italian Night* is my favourite. The connectedness between the characters, the shared history, the gossip, the complex interplay of private and public life: all this is relished, and the weave is luxuriously close. Perhaps Horváth took particular interest in communities where everyone has lived for a long time because he himself was a peripatetic child whose father held various posts in Germany and Austria as Hungarian ambassador. Whatever the reason, in setting out to depict social damage and erosion, he did well to focus on a relatively undisturbed niche like the town in *Italian Night*. What exactly it is that is being damaged and eroded – a fragile ecosystem of habit, decency, conviviality, open-air entertainments – is brilliantly evoked. As are the dormant follies and rivalries which, once stirred, will accelerate the fall of the place.

I like to imagine Horváth lending his own voice to the drunken landlord:

'I'm thinking about my lavatory. You see, originally there was nothing but sex stuff on the walls in there, then during the war it was all patriotism, and now it's all politics – believe what I say, until the day it's all sex again, the German people will never be healthy...'

The landlord is a discredited character who has let the fascists hire his pub. But Horváth doesn't give his 'good' characters a monopoly of truth, or of goodness.

17

The idea of how much is lost when people succumb to the universal temptation to over-simplify is central to Horváth's writing. It permeates his subject matter as well as generating aspects of his social-mosaic technique. There are no slogans in Horváth, no caricatures and rarely a cheap shot. There are interlocking, empirically observed individuals with tragicomically mixed motives.

Everyone in his plays is questionable at some point. *Italian Night* opens with the ultimate reassuring male tableau, a card game in a pub. This begins to unravel as the members of the group try to agree on their response to a threat from outside. Their forthcoming republican 'Italian Night' has had a pall cast over it by the fascists who have chosen the same date for a German Day parade. In the steadily darkening political picture, members of the card game are shown to us individually, in detail, and particularly in relation to their wives and girlfriends. Here, things are more complicated than in cards or in politics. The women emerge from the shadows demanding, with varying degrees of success, personal relationships, a personal life, acting as Horváth's accomplices, refusing to stop articulating ordinary human needs even as slogans and theories take on a frightening life of their own. The abused wife Adele, coming to her pompous republican husband's defence when he in turn is being abused, is the nearest thing in Horváth to a Christ figure, forgiving her enemy. It's typical of Horváth's paradoxical realism that this Christ is a petit bourgeois domestic slave. Martin, the young communist hero who temporarily saves the day by driving off the bullying fascists, is seen to be less than a hero in his relations with the adoring Anna. While Karl, the musician with intellectual pretensions, is rescued from his own inadequacies and from the coming decade of horrors by a girl without a brain in her head.

Meredith Oakes
London 2000

Characters

COUNCILLOR AMMETSBERGER

KRANZ

ENGELBERT

BETZ

LANDLORD

KARL

MARTIN

COMRADES
of Martin

A STRANGE COMRADE FROM MAGDEBURG

THE LIEUTENANT

THE MAJOR

CZERNOWITZ

ADELE

ANNA

LENI

THE DVORAK WOMAN

TWO PROSTITUTES

FRAU HINTERBERGER

THE LEIMSIEDER TWINS

REPUBLICANS

FASCISTS

Setting: A small town in South Germany, 1930 – ?

Scene 1

*In Josef Lehninger's pub. KRANZ, ENGELBERT and
COUNCILLOR AMMETSBERGER are playing Tarock. KARL
looks on. BETZ is quietly drinking his beer. MARTIN reads the
paper. The LANDLORD picks his nose. It is Sunday morning,
and the sun is shining.*

Silence.

BETZ: What's new in the world, Martin?

MARTIN: Nothing. The proletariat are paying taxes and the
    capitalists are fleecing the republic left right and centre, so
    that's nothing new, hey.
    (*BETZ drains his glass.*)
    Also men on pensions paid by the republic are organising
    reactionary imperialist parades with open-air services and
    rifle salutes, while we republicans grin and bear it. So that's
    nothing new either.

BETZ: We're living in a democratic republic, my dear Martin.
    (*Outside, a troop of fascists marches by with music. All except the
    COUNCILLOR and the LANDLORD go to the window and
    silently watch it pass – only when it is gone do they stir again.*)

COUNCILLOR: (*Cards in hand.*) Naturally there's no question
    of a serious threat to the Democratic Republic. Because
    obviously reaction is without any ideological basis.

ENGELBERT: Bravo!

COUNCILLOR: Friends! So long as there exists a Society
    for the Defence of the Republic, and so long as I have the
    honour of being chairman of our local branch here, the
    Republic can sleep soundly!

MARTIN: And good night!

KRANZ: I desire to take the floor! I hereby desire to move
    a motion! I hereby desire to submit that we henceforth
    return to our game of Tarock without letting ourselves be
    any further disturbed either by those Teutonic lackeys or
    by their so-called German Day!

ENGELBERT: Or by their Third Reich!

COUNCILLOR: Carried unanimously! (*He shuffles and deals.*)

KARL: Actually what about this evening?

COUNCILLOR: What about it?

KARL: Well, regarding our Italian Night this evening –

COUNCILLOR: (*Interrupts him.*) Our Italian Night will of course go ahead this evening! Does anyone imagine the Society for the Defence of the Republic would let itself be prevented by any manner of reactionary element from holding an Italian Night here with our friend Josef Lehninger, as and when it chooses? Our republican Italian Night will take place this evening, without regard to Mussolini or any of his kind! Ace of diamonds! (*He leads.*)

ENGELBERT: (*Incredulous.*) Didn't you know that?

KARL: Why would I know it?

BETZ: Because I already officially announced it.

ENGELBERT: Except that Comrade Karl was of course as usual not there. Club!

KARL: I'm not able to be there every time.

ENGELBERT: He wasn't even at the last roll-call, too busy chasing women.

KRANZ: Solo!

COUNCILLOR: Beggar!

ENGELBERT: Already?

COUNCILLOR: Just like that.

KARL: (*To BETZ.*) Am I supposed to stand for that? About chasing women?

BETZ: You can't deny that women are inclined to intervene between you and your duties to the republic –

KARL: My most personal private interests are involved, if you don't mind! If you really don't mind!
(*Another fascist troop passes outside, with music. All listen, but no one goes to the window. Silence.*)

BETZ: Everything's relative, after all.

MARTIN: What? I think it's an out and out disgrace. Reaction is busy arming itself, while we as good republicans hold Italian Nights!

BETZ: It really is surprising how powerful the forces of reaction are getting.

MARTIN: Surprising my arse! It isn't difficult to work it out –
whoever owns the means of production will always be in
the right, it's a known fact. But it doesn't seem to be known
to this committee. I always try to tell myself you want to
know these things, but sometimes I really have trouble –

ENGELBERT: Aha!

BETZ: You're a pessimist.

MARTIN: Pessimist my arse.

COUNCILLOR: In addition to which he's a stirrer, no more
no less than a stirrer.
(*Silence.*)

MARTIN: (*Slowly gets up.*) Councillor. Tell me, Councillor,
have you ever heard of a certain Karl Marx?

COUNCILLOR: (*Bangs the table.*) Of course I know my Marx!
As if I didn't know my Marx! And besides I'm not standing
for this!

ENGELBERT: Quite right!

KRANZ: Solo!

COUNCILLOR: Do you believe, in your shallow deluded
state, that simply with the realisation of Marxism, paradise
will simply arrive on earth?

MARTIN: What you mean by 'simply' I wouldn't know.
I also wouldn't know what you mean by 'paradise', but I
can vividly picture to myself what you mean by 'Marxism'.
Do you understand? What *I* mean by it,
I believe in.

KRANZ: Solo, for Christ's sake! (*He puts out his cards.*)
(*Silence.*)

BETZ: You know what I can't do?

MARTIN: No.

BETZ: Believe.
(*Silence.*)

MARTIN: I can believe you can't believe. You can't believe
because you don't have to. The fact is you're not a member
of the proletariat, you're a former Town Hall secretary –

BETZ: Chief Secretary, not that it matters, naturally.

MARTIN: Naturally.

BETZ: It isn't as natural as all that!

MARTIN: (*Looking at him, startled.*) You can kiss my arse!
(*Goes out quickly, with his newspaper.*)

COUNCILLOR: A delicate man –
(*Silence.*)

LANDLORD: Who thinks it's going to rain again? Every time
I kill a pig, the weather pisses all over my
Italian Nights.

BETZ: I don't think it will.

LANDLORD: Why? Because it's for you lot?

BETZ: No. Because the low over Ireland has given way to a
high over the Bay of Biscay.

COUNCILLOR: Absolutely right!

LANDLORD: And who's claiming this?

BETZ: The official weather report.

LANDLORD: Don't talk to me about officials!
(*MARTIN reappears, goes up to BETZ and puts a handbill down
in front of him.*)

MARTIN: There!

BETZ: What am I supposed to do with that?

MARTIN: Read it!

BETZ: Why should I read that fascist rot?

MARTIN: Because it should interest you.

BETZ: It doesn't in the slightest!

MARTIN: (*Raising his voice.*) What's in it should interest all the
gentlemen present!
(*The GENTLEMEN listen.*)

COUNCILLOR: What's got into him now, our perennial
malcontent?
(*BETZ has been mechanically glancing over the handbill.
He stops short: and now it is he who bangs the table.*)

BETZ: What? But this is disgusting! It's totally
disgusting, Josef!
(*LANDLORD grows nervous and tries to sneak away.
BETZ stares at him furiously.*)
Stop! Stop, dear Josef – what's in here should interest you
most of all – do you know what's written here?

LANDLORD: (*Embarrassed.*) No –

BETZ: You mean you can't read?

LANDLORD: (*Smiles despairingly.*) No –

BETZ: Are you illiterate?

COUNCILLOR: (*Has been listening.*) Just what's all this about?

LANDLORD: Nothing, gentlemen! Nothing –

BETZ: Nothing? But dear Josef, what are you saying?
It seems to me that you're an absolute rogue!

LANDLORD: Don't say that, Heinrich!

BETZ: I'll say it again, dear Josef.

COUNCILLOR: Why's that?

KRANZ: Yes, for God's sake –

MARTIN: (*Interrupts him.*) Hold on!

BETZ: Yes, hold on! What this is, is in fact a so-called Order of
the Day – it's the order of the day for our fascist friends, for
their German Day today – (*He passes the sheet to KARL.*) Josef,
we republicans are your old-established customers, and
here you are selling your soul! For the sake of Mammon!

KARL: But this is gross impertinence! Listen to this, friends!
(*He reads.*) 'From four o'clock to six o'clock the musicians
will forgather in Josef Lehninger's beer garden' –

KRANZ: What musicians?

KARL: The fascist musicians! It's outrageous!

BETZ: It's a disgrace! Our dear Comrade Josef has hired out
our local to the forces of reaction!

KARL: And he's thinking we republicans will come along
with our Italian Night and do him the favour of buying up
his leftovers!

MARTIN: The crumbs from the reactionaries' table!

ENGELBERT: Hear, hear!

LANDLORD: I think we're talking at cross purposes –

MARTIN: What next!

KARL: Ah! If that's not corrupt!

LANDLORD: I'm not corrupt! It isn't me, gentlemen, it's my
wife.

BETZ: Balls!

LANDLORD: It isn't balls! You don't know my wife,
gentlemen! She doesn't give a shit about political
developments. It leaves her quite unmoved who scoffs
down her sausages. And as for me, dumb ox that I am,

I was looking forward to a happy old age! And now if
I don't go and stick out their wretched black, white and red
I'll have sixty portions of roast pork going off on me, what
a piece of nonsense that was, changing the national flag!
My God, I don't know what to do!

KRANZ: If you weren't my friend, dear Josef, what I'd do
now is spit in your face!

ENGELBERT: Bravo!

(*Silence.*)

LANDLORD: (*In despair.*) My God, now I'm going to get
drunk, and then I'll shoot my old woman. After that I think
I'll throw myself out the window, having previously set fire
to the whole establishment. (*Goes.*)

COUNCILLOR: God almighty. Whenever I get a decent
hand, all hell breaks loose! (*Raising his voice.*) But I'd like
to see what power on heaven or earth could put a stop to
our Italian Night this evening! We won't give way, friends,
not even if the whole of world reaction were united against
us! Our republican Italian Night will go ahead this evening
as I've said! No Herr Josef Lehninger is going to put a
spanner in the works! Why don't you all check what hands
you've got, we can carry on playing on my verandah.
Come on, friends!

MARTIN: Hurrah!

KRANZ: You Mephistopheles –

(*All leave the pub.*)

Scene 2

*Street. All the houses are sporting black, white and red flags,
because the local fascist branch has organised, as can be seen from
a banner, a German Day. Right now a troop is passing with flags,
music and small-bore rifles, followed by sections of the patriotically-
minded populace. The DVORAK WOMAN and FRÄULEIN
LENI have also come along.*

LENI: I don't think I can come any further.

THE DVORAK WOMAN: But what a shame, Fräulein!

LENI: I like the music, but I don't really like men in uniform.

They all look the same. And they think they're so
marvellous. Something in me just doesn't accept it.

THE DVORAK WOMAN: I believe you, because after all
you don't remember what it was like before the war.

LENI: I have to go off to the left here.

THE DVORAK WOMAN: Fräulein, there's actually a big
favour you could do me –

LENI: Glad to.

THE DVORAK WOMAN: Your Major must have the most
beautiful uniforms –

LENI: Yes, he does, because he used to be in the colonies too,
before Germany was robbed of them.

THE DVORAK WOMAN: So could you ask the Major if
perhaps he'd like to sell me one of his old uniforms, you
generally get what you want.

LENI: What do you mean by that?

THE DVORAK WOMAN: Well, it's what people say.
(*Silence.*)

LENI: What would you do with a uniform?

THE DVORAK WOMAN: (*Smiles.*) Look at it.

LENI: Just that?

THE DVORAK WOMAN: Make what you will of it –
(*Silence.*)

LENI: I'm sorry, I find that a bit strange –

THE DVORAK WOMAN: (*Flying into a rage.*) You goose, you
silly goose! You young people have simply no illusions!
(*Quickly goes. Drum roll.*)

KARL: (*Comes along and sees LENI.*) Well, what a coincidence!

LENI: Who'd have thought it. Herr Karl!

KARL: It is, though, undoubtedly.

LENI: How do you mean?

KARL: Meeting here by pure chance like this.

LENI: I don't know, it often happens.

KARL: Undoubtedly.
(*Silence.*)

LENI: I don't have much time now, Herr Karl!

KARL: I don't either. But there's something I'd like to suggest,
Fräulein.

LENI: So what would you like to suggest?

KARL: I'd like to suggest that we two attractive young people could maybe see each other tonight – I would have suggested it yesterday, but there just wasn't any opportunity –

LENI: Don't tell such lies, Herr Karl.

(*Silence.*)

KARL: (*Bows abruptly.*) Dear lady. I've never yet found it necessary to lie to a woman, because after all I'm an honourable person, please bear that in mind!

LENI: I didn't mean to offend you –

KARL: You couldn't.

LENI: (*Stares at him.*) What do you mean by that, Herr Karl?

KARL: I mean, you couldn't offend me because I like you – what you could do, Fräulein, is hurt me. That's what I mean. Forgive me!

(*Silence.*)

LENI: I think you're quite bad.

KARL: There are no bad people, Fräulein. There are only very unfortunate people. Forgive me!

(*Silence.*)

LENI: I'll only wait ten minutes –

KARL: I'll only wait five.

LENI: All right, bad person – (*Goes.*)

(*MARTIN and BETZ enter. MARTIN gazes after LENI, who has walked quickly past him; then he looks quizzically at KARL.*)

KARL: Tell me, Martin: I assume of course our Italian Night this evening will welcome not just registered ordinary and extraordinary members but also sympathisers –

MARTIN: Nothing to do with me.

KARL: Only I've just invited someone. Someone known to me as a sympathiser of mine.

MARTIN: Was that her?

KARL: Do you know her?

MARTIN: Yes, unfortunately.

KARL: How's that?

MARTIN: She's a very obstinate woman.

KARL: Still I find she has a certain something.

MARTIN: Of course she has a certain something – her certain something isn't what I'm talking about! I mean she's a woman who's politically extremely obstinate, for God's sake, a born reactionary. How could anyone go out with that!

KARL: My dear Martin, you don't understand. You and I are both good republicans, but there's also a difference between us. Namely, that you're a worker, and I'm a musician. You're standing, in a sense, on the production line while I'm in the cafe playing my Mozart and my Kalman; because of this I'm naturally more of an individualist, simply because I possess artistic sensibilities. I have stronger personal concerns, although only apparently, because with me everything is immediately transmuted to the realm of art.

MARTIN: (*Grins.*) You and your fancy excuses.

KARL: What I owe to myself, simply, is that in the erotic sense I should be able to lead a politically non-aligned existence – Forgive me! (*Goes.*)

MARTIN: Go to it.

(*Silence.*)

BETZ: Martin, you know how highly I think of you, despite the fact that you're sometimes disagreeably bad-tempered – I think you're overlooking something very important in your assessment of the political situation worldwide, namely the role of love-life in nature. I've recently been coming to grips, I should tell you, with the works of Professor Freud. You shouldn't forget that all around the Ego are grouped aggressive drives which are continually at war with our Eros, and which express themselves for example as the drive to commit suicide, or else as sadism, masochism, sex, murder –

MARTIN: What have your perversions got to do with me, you dirty beast?

BETZ: They're yours as well!

MARTIN: You don't say!

BETZ: Haven't you ever given your Anna a bite or something when you – I mean to say: at the crucial moment – ?

MARTIN: It's sod-all to do with you.

BETZ: And then, you see, they're not perversions at all, they're just basic drives! I tell you our aggressive drives play an immensely important role in the realisation of socialism, namely in the form of inhibition. I'm afraid that in this respect you're pursuing the policy of the ostrich.

MARTIN: For the second time today, you know what you can do. (*Leaves him standing.*)

Scene 3

In the municipal gardens. Many flags. The air is full of military music. Two PROSTITUTES are standing on the corner. It is already late afternoon. The COUNCILLOR walks past. The PROSTITUTES wink.

FIRST PROSTITUTE: (*Old and withered.*) Do you know him?

SECOND PROSTITUTE: (*Young and fat.*) He's all right.

FIRST PROSTITUTE: He's something in the Town Hall I think. Some big shot.

SECOND PROSTITUTE: I expect so.

(*The flags wave in the wind.*)

SECOND PROSTITUTE: (*Looks up.*) If only those flags weren't there –

FIRST PROSTITUTE: Flags are very uplifting though.

SECOND PROSTITUTE: Not really – when I see flags like that I feel as if the war were still on.

FIRST PROSTITUTE: (*Putting on lipstick.*) I've nothing against the World War. That would be ungrateful.

(*Silence.*)

SECOND PROSTITUTE: (*Still looking up.*) Look at them all flapping – what good are they to us?

FIRST PROSTITUTE: For me the best is agricultural shows, or even better, cultural events. But patriotic ceremonies are all right.

(*A FASCIST goes by. The FIRST PROSTITUTE goes up to him.*)

FASCIST: Stand back!

(*Pause.*)

SECOND PROSTITUTE: Actually the war's responsible.

FIRST PROSTITUTE: What for?

SECOND PROSTITUTE: Me.

FIRST PROSTITUTE: What a joke! Everyone's always blaming the poor old war!
(ANNA comes and sits on a bench with her back to the two PROSTITUTES; she waits.)
Who's that?

SECOND PROSTITUTE: I don't know her.

FIRST PROSTITUTE: She looks so new. Yet she reminds me of someone –

SECOND PROSTITUTE: *(Grins.)* You –

FIRST PROSTITUTE: *(Stares at her.)* Now that was cheap of you, Agnes.
(Three FASCISTS walk towards ANNA. ANNA looks away. The FASCISTS stop in front of her and grin. ANNA gets up and starts to walk away. MARTIN appears in front of her, greets her briefly and speaks with her. The FASCISTS and the PROSTITUTES listen but can't hear.)

ANNA: And?

MARTIN: There isn't any and. Our Councillor wriggled out of it as usual. He said it was beneath his honour as a republican to forgo his Italian Night either for them and their German Day or for the odious Lehninger. He's a cut-price copy of the typical MP. Whatever happens, that's what was meant to happen.

ANNA: The man's corrupt.

MARTIN: Profit rules, so the antisocial elements have the upper hand. And they've created a world in their own image. But I guarantee, tonight at their Italian Night they'll get one dance more that they bargained for! As a friendly reminder.
(The FASCISTS are occupying themselves with the PROSTITUTES.)

ANNA: Do you know what the comrades say?

MARTIN: What?

ANNA: That you've got a future.

MARTIN: *(Shrugs his shoulders.)* They know me, don't they.
But I'd have to go away. To some big city.

ANNA: I have that feeling too, that people are waiting for you.

MARTIN: My sphere of action is much too small here. What I do here could be done by anyone.

ANNA: No, no one could do what you do!

MARTIN: You know I don't like you saying that.

ANNA: But it's true. If everyone were like you, the world would be better.

MARTIN: I can't help being as I am. The fact that I'm more intelligent and able to see things through just makes it my duty to work harder for what I believe in! I don't want to hear any more about being an exception. Christ! (*He shouts at her.*) I'm not one, so remember it!

ANNA: All right, you're not an exception, only couldn't you find a different way of saying so?

(*Silence.*)

MARTIN: Anna, time's rushing on, and there are more burning problems in the world than matters of form. Remember your commitments.

ANNA: Me?

MARTIN: Commitments commit.

ANNA: Martin, now you're talking as if I were a person who didn't honour their commitments –

MARTIN: What makes you think that? You've misunderstood. Don't start complicating the simplest things! I only wanted to remind you what we talked about the day before yesterday – so please will you do it? Yes? (*Goes.*)

(*Meanwhile two FASCISTS have disappeared with the PROSTITUTES. The third FASCIST stares at ANNA.*)

ANNA: Well?

(*The third FASCIST grins. She smiles.*)

Well?

(*KARL appears behind the FASCIST. ANNA starts.*)

KARL: Forgive me!

(*The third FASCIST grins; bows to ANNA with mock elegance and leaves. Silence. KARL suppresses his agitation.*)

Forgive me, esteemed lady!

ANNA: You fool!

KARL: God. Anna with a fascist, a world's collapsing inside me – tell me who's crazy, me or you?

ANNA: You! I was trying so hard to get started, and now you've blundered in all over everything, you inconsiderate idiot!

KARL: Inconsiderate!

ANNA: And irresponsible!

KARL: Irresponsible! Martin chews me up for fancying a non-political woman, while his one's busy picking up a fascist – my God, now I really do believe it, I'm mad! Definitely mad! I'm a head case!

ANNA: Would you please calm down!

KARL: Oh my poor Martin!

ANNA: But I wouldn't do anything without Martin!

KARL: (*Stares at her.*) What?

ANNA: I'm doing absolutely nothing wrong!

KARL: Really?

ANNA: It's all completely all right – only Martin wants more exact information about their rifles – so I'm supposed to befriend a fascist and get him to talk –
(*Silence. KARL lights a cigarette.*)
What did you think?

KARL: Me? Forgive me!

ANNA: That's so insulting –

KARL: Forgive me!

ANNA: You should be ashamed!
(*Silence.*)

KARL: Anna. I've had quite a lot of experience in sexual matters, and after a while one gets a bit cynical. Especially if one's a keen observer, as I am. Naturally you possess moral greatness. Anyway, you've changed a lot.

ANNA: (*Smiles.*) Thanks.

KARL: Not at all. But in fact you were different. Before.

ANNA: (*Nods.*) Yes, before.

KARL: You weren't so puritanical then.
(*Silence.*)

ANNA: (*Suddenly serious.*) And?

KARL: Seeing you like this gives a jolt to my conscience. Martin's quite right, one shouldn't let oneself go – I'm meeting someone here in a minute, she's totally uninterested in politics – (*Looks at his watch.*)

ANNA: Then if I were you I'd try to be a good influence on her.

KARL: God I will! I promise!

ANNA: How many times have you said that before?

KARL: Anna. It's more important to see into one's faults than it is to reject them as faults. What if I were to promise you that at our Italian Night this evening I'll practise passive resistance, in a sense?

ANNA: What am I supposed to understand by that?

KARL: Well, for instance: I won't dance a single dance. Word of honour! Not a step! Not even with her! After all there's no sense charging through life like a brute beast, always thinking only of satisfying one's baser instincts –

(*He involuntarily puts his arm around her waist, not noticing what he's doing. ANNA slowly takes his hand away and gives him a long look. KARL becomes aware of what he's done. Silence. Nastily.*)

But I do think it's strange of Martin.

ANNA: What?

KARL: I could never do it –

ANNA: What, then?

KARL: I can't picture to myself the way in which he loves you. I mean, whether it's normal, whether it's as it should be –

ANNA: What are you talking about?

KARL: Just that it interests me. In fact by asking you to do something like this he's in a sense using you as a political whore – I wonder if he has inner conflicts about that?

ANNA: Inner conflicts?

KARL: Yes!

(*Silence.*)

ANNA: No he doesn't! You won't confuse me! I know Martin better than that! He stands above all of us. I used to be dull, stupid, dishonest, small-minded, and horrible – he pulled me out of it. I was never happy with myself. Now I am.

(*KARL gives a little bow.*)

Now I've got something to me, you know? (*She slowly walks off.*)

KARL: Forgive me! (*Looks at his watch, walks up and down, waiting.*)

LENI: (*Arriving.*) Good evening, Herr Karl! I'm just glad you're still here. Unfortunately I couldn't get here any sooner!

KARL: We've still got time. And anyway, people don't look any the worse for coming later.

LENI: Why so sad then?

KARL: Sad?

LENI: Your voice – like from the tomb. (*She smiles.*)

KARL: I've just had an experience. I mean a political experience. We should be more aware of the issues of the day, Fräulein. I think there's a curse on me.

LENI: But Herr Karl! When a person's got such a nice walk! (*She laughs.*)

KARL: What?

(*He stares at her. LENI is struck dumb. Silence.*)
Fräulein, you don't seem to understand me. It would take me hours to explain it to you, actually – the future looks black, Fräulein.

LENI: Go on, you're a man –

KARL: It's precisely as a man one's bound to despair all the sooner, particularly me, because I'm closer to the political events of our time – you're not interested in politics?

LENI: No.

KARL: But you should be.

LENI: Why are you talking about all of this now?

KARL: In your own best interests.

LENI: Are you trying to make me angry?

KARL: It's actually your duty as a citizen –

LENI: Why do you want to spoil my whole mood, I was really looking forward to your Italian Night!
(*Silence.*)

KARL: I'm not made in such a way that I can just pluck a flower by the wayside. I need some kind of human contact as well – and with me it takes the form of politics.

LENI: Go on, you don't believe that yourself!

KARL: But I do! For example, in the long run I couldn't ever get along with a woman who had a different world view.

LENI: All you men have the same world view.
(*Silence.*)

KARL: But you're a German?

LENI: Yes.

KARL: Look, Fräulein, it's the besetting sin of us Germans
that we don't concern ourselves with politics, we're not
a political nation – we've still got masses of people who
haven't the faintest idea who governs them.

LENI: It's all the same to me as well. It isn't getting any better.
I'm just going to see to it that I come through.

KARL: It seems to me you have no solidarity.

LENI: Don't talk down your nose to me like that!

KARL: It seems to me you might not even know who the
Reichspresident is.

LENI: I don't remember people's names!

KARL: I bet you don't know who's the Reichschancellor.

LENI: I don't know that either.

KARL: But that's monstrous! And again, typically German! Could
you imagine a Frenchwoman not knowing those things?

LENI: So go to France!

(*Silence.*)

KARL: Who's the Minister of the Interior? Or else how many
ministers would you say we have? Approximately?

LENI: If you don't stop I'll walk off and leave you here!

KARL: Unbelievable!

(*Silence.*)

LENI: I imagined this evening quite differently.

KARL: Me too.

LENI: A person goes out for once – and then they get their
head bitten off.

KARL: (*Looks at his watch.*) It's nearly time.

LENI: I'd just as soon not go.

(*KARL suddenly puts his arms round her and gives her a kiss.
LENI doesn't resist.*)

KARL: (*Looks deep into her eyes and smiles a pain-laden smile.*)
Yes, the Minister of the Interior – (*Pulls her close again.*)

Scene 4

*In the municipal gardens, in front of the statue of the former Emperor.
Two LADS (MARTIN's COMRADES) are painting the emperor's
face red. A third LAD is lookout. It's getting quite dark. Far in
the distance the fascists are playing the 'Bavarian Präsentiermarsch'.*

FIRST LAD: In the morning they'll see how much His
Majesty has changed – His Majesty's face will have got
extremely red – blood-red –

SECOND LAD: Look at him staring proudly in front of him!

FIRST LAD: (*Slaps a brushful of paint in His Majesty's face.*) It's a
pity in a way he's only got one head!

THIRD LAD: Stop!

SECOND LAD: Hey?

THIRD LAD: Christ, there are two just coming!

SECOND LAD: Let's go.

FIRST LAD: Finished!

(*Leaves quickly with his friends. It will soon be completely dark.
ANNA arrives with a FASCIST.*)

FASCIST: Your town here's a really beautiful town, Fräulein.
As a child of this town it must fill you with really special
pride.

ANNA: Yes, I'm proud I'm from here.

FASCIST: Honour your homeland! And these are very ap-
propriate gardens you have here.

ANNA: Don't you want to sit down?

FASCIST: Permission granted! (*They sit down.*)

ANNA: I'm rather tired in fact, I've been following the bands
all day.

FASCIST: So you too have martial music in your blood?

ANNA: I think I do have it in my blood – (*She lies.*) My father
was actually a sergeant-major on active service!

FASCIST: Atten-shun!

(*Silence.*)

That's the big statue of His Majesty up there, is it?

ANNA: Yes.

FASCIST: I've already had the honour of getting to know it.
We had an internal group discussion here this morning –
it really is a lovely statue, a lot of style. Unfortunately it's
already got so dark we can no longer admire it!

ANNA: Was your internal group discussion very important?

FASCIST: Very much so.

ANNA: So what did you discuss?

FASCIST: Our mission – it isn't true when mercenary slaves
to money say we came into this world just to suffer, to

consume and to die! We have a mission to fulfil! Some feel the drive more strongly, it's weaker in others. In us it burns like sacrificial fire! We shall go on to the bitter end! (*Silence.*)

ANNA: There's something I'd like to know.

FASCIST: Any time!

ANNA: I'm not really very up with politics and I don't know much about your movement yet –

FASCIST: (*Interrupts her.*) Woman belongs to hearth and home, she must comfort and help the warrior.

ANNA: Only there's something I wanted to know about the future, just roughly –

FASCIST: Fräulein, don't ply me with questions, I beg you. I mustn't speak of that, because it's a deep, sacred secret. (*Silence.*)
What arrant nonsense it is, when they say we're not a party of the proletariat! I know what I'm talking about. I'm among the better educated and by no means the most stupid! I'm a pharmacist!

ANNA: It's getting dark.

FASCIST: (*Hollowly.*) Yes, dark. (*Silence.*)
Dark, as it is here inside me. Fräulein, I can hardly see you – your blonde hair –

ANNA: I'm not blonde, I'm brunette.

FASCIST: Dark blonde, dark blonde – beware little blonde girl, beware! You know of whom – The Jew was the one who took us into war! 1914 was the time for him! Because a time could have come when nations stooped being hard of hearing. Suppose an epidemic had broken out worldwide, then people would have quickly understood it was the Jews who were to blame! Blonde girl, it fills me with joy that you let me approach you –

ANNA: I don't usually let people come up to me like that, but –

FASCIST: But?

ANNA: But someone like you – no, don't – please don't – let me go, please.

FASCIST: Of course. At your service!

(*Silence.*)

ANNA: I can't, straight away like that.

FASCIST: But it isn't straight away! We've had quite a long
talk, first concerning art, then your beautiful town and just
now about the rebirth of our nation –
(*Silence. He suddenly rounds on her.*)
And do you know, by the way, who's dragged us under?
Materialism! I'll tell you how it's got hold of us, I know
a bit about it. For twenty-three years, you see, my father
has run his own business. This is how it was, you see.
Whenever we came along, the Jew had been there before
us and bought everything up. He just came in, you see, and
ripped out all the bargains. In this way everyone's been
swept into the vortex and in this way, isn't it the case, the
spirit of materialism has been spreading wider and wider.
But the problem is we've become too effeminate! It's time
for us to put our trousers back on and remember we're
Cimbrians and Teutons! (*He throws himself on her.*)

ANNA: Stop it! No! (*Defends herself.*)
(*Now the statue is lit up, and His Majesty is seen with a red face.*)

FASCIST: (*Hoarsely; lets go of ANNA.*) What? No, this
desecration – this desecration – God who made iron –
Vengeance! – God be with us – Germany awake!
(*In the distance, the 'Hakenkreuzlied'.*)

Scene 5

*In Josef Lehninger's beer garden. With music. The FASCISTS are
drinking beer and singing*:

FASCISTS: I wander heavy-hearted
   Oppressed against my will
   From ages long departed
   A legend haunts me still.
   The air is cool in the twilight
   And softly flows the Rhine – *

FASCIST: The Rhine, the Rhine, The German Rhine –

* *'Die Lorelei'*

ALL: Defenders are we all of thine!
Fear not, dear Fatherland of mine,
Fear not, dear Fatherland of mine,
Firm stands and true the watch, the watch on the Rhine,
Firm stands and true the watch, the watch on the Rhine!

FASCISTS: (*With beer mugs in hand.*) Heil! Heil! Heil!
(*They drink. Now the music is: 'Proud Waves the Flag Black White and Red'.*)

THE LIEUTENANT: (*With map; he summons a FASCIST over to him.*) So, our night exercise. Behind this marsh lies France for example, right next to the Anglo-Saxon artillery. Bolsheviks above and below. You understand?

FASCIST: Yes, sir.

THE LIEUTENANT: And where are we? We're here in the forest. German forest. It's quite symbolic really. Obviously we're attacked. Throughout world history it can be seen that we Germans have never yet wronged another nation. So let's just suppose the whole world were against us –

LANDLORD: Excuse me please!

THE LIEUTENANT: Herr Lehninger!

LANDLORD: Herr Leutnant, I'm actually needing my beer garden now –

THE LIEUTENANT: What's that supposed to mean?

LANDLORD: It's getting near the time – you need to leave my beer garden now –

THE LIEUTENANT: Good lord, how dare you?

LANDLORD: Only it's my duty as a patriot to remind you – otherwise you might miss your various night exercises – (*Silence.*)

THE LIEUTENANT: (*Waves the FASCIST away; calls.*) Czernowitz!

CZERNOWITZ: (*A schoolboy.*) Present, Herr Leutnant!

THE LIEUTENANT: The Major's waiting for us in the forest. The Major's going to read his lecture in our German forest. Is the lecture ready?

CZERNOWITZ: It is, Herr Leutnant! (*Passes him some sheets from an exercise book.*)

THE LIEUTENANT: Title?

CZERNOWITZ: 'Why Should We Germans Be Grateful
To The Japanese?'

THE LIEUTENANT: Correct – why didn't you copy it out
neatly, boy?

CZERNOWITZ: You don't know my father, Herr Leutnant!
He cares for nothing except my schoolwork! My family
don't understand me, Herr Leutnant. Recently, when
I said I was happy we had so many enemies, because it's
an honour, father punched me. If I didn't have mother,
Herr Leutnant – mother's the only one who understands
me, you see – father's a liberal.
(*Silence.*)

LIEUTENANT: Dismiss!
(*CZERNOWITZ turns away.*)
Fall in!
(*The FASCISTS fall in.*)
Attention! Right turn! Unit – march!
(*The FASCISTS march off. The 'Bavarian Präsentiermarsch'
plays. The LANDLORD takes down the black, white and red
flag and runs up the black, red and gold one.*
*Now it is dark, and now begins the republican Italian
Night. With garlands and Chinese lanterns, brass music and
dancing. Members and sympathisers arrive in the beer garden
with music: 'March of the Gladiators'; the COUNCILLOR
at their head, KRANZ, BETZ, ENGELBERT, all with
their wives. KARL and LENI are there. And MARTIN
comes in with his COMRADES, scowling and looking
determined – they sit together off to one side.*)

COUNCILLOR: Ladies and gentlemen! Comrades! Just a few
hours ago it seemed as if the fates, so adversely inclined
towards us humans, and not least towards us republicans,
intended our heart's desire, our long-awaited dream, our
Italian Night not to become a reality. Comrades! In the
name of the committee I bring you the welcome news
that we have battled the fates and won! When I see the
magnificent atmosphere that has been created here, the
happiness and expectation on every face, both young and
old, it makes me fully aware of what a victory has been

achieved! So I'd like to express the wish that this our open-air event, our republican Italian Night, will be for everyone present an unforgettable one! Three cheers for the United Republic of the German People! Hurrah! Hurrah! Hurrah!

ALL: (*All except MARTIN's COMRADES stand up.*) Hurrah! Hurrah! Hurrah!

(*Flourish of music.*)

COUNCILLOR: Please be seated!

ENGELBERT: Ladies and gentlemen! Comrades! Delightful sympathisers! I'm glad we're all here! Take your partners for the Française!

(*The COUNCILLOR, BETZ, KRANZ etc. and their wives dance the 'Française' – MARTIN and his COMRADES watch darkly. Now the music changes to a waltz.*) Ladies' choice! Ladies' choice!

MARTIN: (*To his COMRADES.*) No-one take it into his head to dance please – I must have discipline – discipline and resistance.

(*Some girls ask to dance with MARTIN's COMRADES but are refused.*)

LENI: (*To KARL.*) So could I have the honour? (*KARL remains silent.*) So for the last time, could I have the honour? (*KARL remains silent.*) How anyone could let themselves be begged by a girl –

KARL: Do you think I'm finding it easy?

LENI: What are we here for then, if we're not going to dance?

KARL: It has a deeper significance.

LENI: You call yourself a man? And won't even dare to have one dance?

KARL: As a man, one can take back many things, but not one's word of honour.

LENI: A real man can do anything. No, take your hand away.

KARL: What hand?

LENI: Your hand.

KARL: You simply don't know what it is to have conflicts – otherwise you wouldn't be putting this kind of pressure on me – (*He starts involuntarily to dance with her; counterclockwise.*)

FIRST COMRADE: Look Martin, he gave Anna his word he was with us –

MARTIN: He pledged his word to Anna he wouldn't dance a step and he'd totally take his cue from us.

SECOND COMRADE: He's a write-off, no character at all.

THIRD COMRADE: Another one.

FIRST COMRADE: And every time, it's because of a woman –

FOURTH COMRADE: She doesn't half fancy herself!

THIRD COMRADE: Lady Muck!

FIRST COMRADE: That one'll never know what solidarity means!

SECOND COMRADE: Who is the woman, in fact?

FOURTH COMRADE: A worker.

FIRST COMRADE: On the contrary. It's someone far more exalted. It's a servant –

(*He grins. The THIRD COMRADE laughs.*)

FOURTH COMRADE: So when shall we do it?

(*The THIRD COMRADE suddenly stops laughing.*)

MARTIN: When I give you the signal! Me, no one else!

(*MARTIN gets up, goes over to the dancers and watches. A waltz is playing. A few couples stop dancing, among them the COUNCILLOR.*)

COUNCILLOR: How about this for an idea?

ENGELBERT: It's a brilliant idea!

COUNCILLOR: I knew for a fact that an informal social get-together would bring us republicans closer as human beings.

KRANZ: (*Slightly drunk.*) I'm only glad we didn't let ourselves be intimidated by those shits of reactionaries, and also that we were able to dismiss the complete spinelessness of our dear Josef with a careless wave of the hand. It speaks of inner greatness.

COUNCILLOR: An excellent idea!

ENGELBERT: A propaganda victory!

KRANZ: Those bloody fascists would be more than a little put out, if they could see us republicans now in such free and easy vein! (*He reels a bit.*)

ENGELBERT: Where have the fascists got to now, then?

BETZ: I heard something about night exercises.

ENGELBERT: They're welcome.

KRANZ: Cheers!

COUNCILLOR: All this childish fooling about with rifles.

BETZ: Though it's said they've got machine guns also –

COUNCILLOR: Talk, idle talk! No faint hearts now, comrades. Allow me to introduce my wife, my better half!

KRANZ: Most delighted!

ENGELBERT: A pleasure!

BETZ: We know each other by sight.

(*The better half smiles uncertainly.*)

COUNCILLOR: Is that so? Where do you know each other from?

BETZ: I saw you out walking with her.

COUNCILLOR: Me? With her? We never go anywhere.

BETZ: I did though. In fact it must have been just before Christmas –

COUNCILLOR: You're right! It was her birthday! The one day of the year she comes along with me, to the cinema. (*He smiles and pinches her cheek.*) Her name's Adele. Today's an exception in fact, a big exception – Adele doesn't like being out in public, she prefers to be at home. (*He grins.*) A little housemother.

KRANZ: (*To ADELE.*) Home and hearth. Where-e'er I may wander there's no place like home. The family is the back-bone of the state. What finer songs than these, the lovely Viennese. (*He staggers about humming into his beer.*)

BETZ: He's a scamp.

ENGELBERT: (*To ADELE.*) May I have the honour?

COUNCILLOR: No thank you! Adele shouldn't dance. She perspires.

(*Pause. ENGELBERT dances with a girl of fifteen.*)

ADELE: (*Timidly.*) Alfons!

COUNCILLOR: What?

ADELE: I don't perspire.

COUNCILLOR: Leave these things to me, please.

ADELE: So why am I not supposed to dance?

COUNCILLOR: You can't dance!

ADELE: Me? Of course I can dance!

COUNCILLOR: Since when?

ADELE: Since always!

COUNCILLOR: You've never been able to dance! Even as
a young girl you couldn't, please note! Don't show me up,
Madam Councillor! (*He lights a cigar.*)
(*Pause.*)

ADELE: Alfons, why did you say I don't like going out in public? I used to go with you quite often. Why did you say that?

COUNCILLOR: Because.
(*Pause.*)

ADELE: I know you're in public life, a public figure –

COUNCILLOR: Silence, Madam Councillor!

ADELE: You're always putting me in a false light. It's you that
tells me not to come with you –

COUNCILLOR: (*Interrupts her.*) Can't you see!

ADELE: (*Nastily.*) See what?

COUNCILLOR: That you drag me down.
(*Pause.*)

ADELE: I'd like never to go anywhere again.

COUNCILLOR: Good idea! (*He turns away from her. To BETZ.*)
My wife, hey? (*He grins and threatens her roguishly with his fore-
finger.*) When going to the women, don't forget your whip.

BETZ: Nietzsche said that.

COUNCILLOR: Who cares who said it! It's her to the letter.
Isn't this a marvellous place! The ancient trees and the air
full of ozone – (*He breathes deeply.*)

BETZ: Yes, well such are the wonders of nature.

COUNCILLOR: The wonders of creation – there's nothing
more extraordinary. I can vouch for it, I was a farmer's
son. Looking up into the heavens like this, one feels so
infinitesimally small – those eternal stars! What are we
compared with them?

BETZ: Nothing!

COUNCILLOR: Nothing. God certainly does have wonderful
taste.

BETZ: Everything's relative, after all.
(*Silence.*)

COUNCILLOR: You know, Betz, I've bought myself a block
of land.

BETZ: Where?

COUNCILLOR: Best part of an acre. With some of it cleared. You see, my good friend, the world has room for one and a half billion people, why shouldn't I possess a tiny corner of this great big world?

FIRST COMRADE: (*Hasn't been able to help overhearing.*) Some Marxist!

(*Silence.*)

COUNCILLOR: What did he say?

BETZ: Oh, never mind him!

ADELE: He said, some Marxist.

COUNCILLOR: The way you say that, right in my face – That's really something!

ADELE: I'm only saying what he said.

COUNCILLOR: Who? The things these little twerps come out with. Marvellous. (*Indicates MARTIN and COMRADES.*) Not one of them dancing – clean-living youth. Anything and everything, they're against it. Rebellion and the like. Splinter groups. In need of authority. We have to – (*He's heading towards his own table, but stops as he sees that MARTIN and his COMRADES are quietly debating something among themselves. He tries to hear – suddenly walks quickly over to MARTIN.*) Martin, what was that you said? Some Marxist, did you say?

MARTIN: I didn't say it actually, but I could have said it.

COUNCILLOR: If you'd said it, what would you have meant by it?

MARTIN: We'll discuss it some time. (*He leaves him standing.*)

(*Chord and gong.*)

ENGELBERT: (*On the podium.*) Ladies and gentlemen! Friends! I bring you a tremendous and wonderful surprise. We're in for an exceptional artistic treat. Frau Hinterberger, wife of our much-loved and respected treasurer, has kindly indicated her willingness to delight us with her contralto voice!

(*Applause, bravos.*)

Pray silence for Frau Hinterberger.

FRAU HINTERBERGER: (*Steps onto the podium, greeted by applause.*) I should like to sing you a ballad by Lowe,

'Heinrich der Vogler'.
(*She sings the ballad; great applause, except that MARTIN and his COMRADES, as before, do not take part in any ovation. The dancing resumes.*)

LENI: (*To KARL.*) That was lovely. I'm very musical you know.

KARL: Yes, I've noticed.

LENI: How did you notice?

KARL: From your dancing. You have quite an incredible sense of rhythm –

LENI: It isn't just me. It depends on the man as well.

KARL: So you're not sorry you came along with me?

LENI: (*Smiles.*) Only don't go all political on me again – Promise me you never will, on your honour.

KARL: It's not so easy.

LENI: Why not?

KARL: Well, I only like to give a promise if I'm in a position to keep it. Promises are easier to break than keep.

LENI: If you promise, I'll promise you something too –

KARL: Will you?

LENI: A woman hasn't got much to give – but what she gives can make a man a king.

MARTIN: (*To KARL.*) Karl, could I speak to you for a minute?

KARL: If you like. (*To LENI.*) Forgive me! (*To MARTIN.*) Well?

MARTIN: You promised Anna, didn't you, that you wouldn't dance – so; I'd just like to point out that you've broken with your political faith for the sake of your own pleasures.

KARL: (*Grows nervous.*) Have I?

MARTIN: Yes. You also promised me that when it came to the ideological confrontation which is now impending –

KARL: (*Interrupts him.*) Yes, I did, so please don't go all moral again.

MARTIN: Only once again you've tarnished your honour.

KARL: Are you serious?

MARTIN: Very, Mr Artistic Sensibilities –
(*Pause.*)

KARL: (*Smiles nastily.*) Martin, where's Anna got to?

MARTIN: What do you mean?

KARL: I assume she'll appear?

MARTIN: Did you see her?

KARL: Yes.

MARTIN: Alone or with?

KARL: With.

MARTIN: (*Smiles.*) So that's good.

KARL: You think?

MARTIN: Yes.

(*Pause.*)

KARL: (*Grins.*) *Honi soit qui mal y pense!*

MARTIN: What does that mean?

KARL: (*With malicious relish.*) It's French.

(*Pause.*)

MARTIN: I'm not angry with you, I'm sorry for you. It's a shame about you, with the talents you've got. All you ever do is make excuses. Half a man – (*Leaves him standing.*) (*Chord and gong.*)

ENGELBERT: (*On the podium.*) Honoured guests! Friends! Once more I bring you a tremendous and delightful surprise in our programme! In the course of our artistic offerings there now follows a special ballet performed by none other than the lovely twin daughters of our own Comrade Leimsieder, entitled 'Flower and Butterfly'.

(*The lovely TWIN DAUGHTERS, thirteen years old, mount the podium to loud applause.*)

COUNCILLOR: Bravo, Leimsieder!

(*The lovely TWIN DAUGHTERS perform a dance that is affected and kitsch – suddenly from MARTIN's quarter a shrill whistle is heard. The lovely TWIN DAUGHTERS are startled but continue to dance, albeit now somewhat uncertainly; some of the guests choose to look furiously towards MARTIN – another whistle is heard, shriller than the first.*)

KRANZ: (*Bellows.*) Silence, for Christ's sake. Who's that whistling, you snot-nosed little brats? Nasty brainless louts!

ENGELBERT: If you don't like it, why don't you get out?

(*Calls of 'Out, out'. Tumult. The lovely TWIN DAUGHTERS are weeping loudly.*)

FIRST COMRADE: (*Bangs the table with his fist.*) We don't want babies' ballet!

KRANZ: I said shut up.

SECOND COMRADE: Shut up yourself!

AN AUNT: Look how the kids are crying, you brutes!

THIRD COMRADE: Imperial Theatre!

FOURTH COMRADE: Imperial Opera! Opera!

COUNCILLOR: This is too ridiculous!

SOME COMRADES: Boo!

COUNCILLOR: I'm very energetic!

COMRADES: Boo!

COUNCILLOR: There'll be a reckoning!

THIRD COMRADE: Dee da dee da!

AUNT: Oh, young people today!

FOURTH COMRADE: Some Marxist!

COMRADES: (*In chorus.*) Some Marxist! Some Marxist! Some Marxist! Some Marxist!

COUNCILLOR: Who? Me? I had the Communist Manifesto off by heart when you were still in nappies, you yobs! (*Whistle.*)

AUNT: Barbarians, they're just destroying the artistic experience.

FOURTH COMRADE: You and your artistic experience!

THIRD COMRADE: 'Flower and Butterfly'.

FIRST COMRADE: Rubbish, rubbish, rubbish!

KRANZ: (*Almost falling over from drunkenness.*) You artistic ignoramuses!

ENGELBERT: See what you've done! Children's tears! Aren't you ashamed of yourselves? Have you got the slightest idea how much love went into preparing all this – for weeks and weeks Comrade Leimsieder and his wife have given up every spare minute for the sake of tonight's enjoyment!

A STRANGE COMRADE FROM MAGDEBURG: Better if he'd given up his spare minutes to strengthening this organisation's striking power! (*A deathly hush*: *boundless surprise over the strange accent.*)

COUNCILLOR: Ah, a Prussian – (*Storm.*)

THE DVORAK WOMAN: Stop interfering in our night!

MARTIN: A night like this deserves to be interfered with!

STRANGE COMRADE: Comrades!

MARTIN: I'm speaking! Comrades! While we've been organising family get-togethers with republican child ballets, the reactionaries have set up a military night exercise with machine guns!

STRANGE COMRADE: Comrades and women comrades! Can you refuse to see how they're thumbing their noses, lying and stealing from the proletariat worse than they ever did? And you?

MARTIN: (*Interrupts him.*) And you? Italian Nights! Have you forgotten the words, 'Oh, would that every worker found his pleasure in republican – '

STRANGE COMRADE: (*Interrupts him.*) In revolutionary! 'In revolutionary activity!' It only remains to call for –

COUNCILLOR: Nothing remains to call for!

MARTIN: It only remains to call for an immediate emergency meeting of the committee to vote on the resolution!

STRANGE COMRADE: Arming with small-bore rifles!

KRANZ: Shut up, you filthy damned Prussian!
(*Calls of 'Get him out! Out!'*)

STRANGE COMRADE: Women comrades and comrades!

MARTIN: I'm speaking, for Christ's sake! You'll make me lose the thread completely! I want the same thing, but we'll never get anywhere like this! So will you let the existing leader speak?

COUNCILLOR: Friends! This vandal dares to upset our festivities, and makes small children cry – Friends, what Martin is demanding is not practicable! We have no wish to follow in the footsteps of reaction. We are not about to start going around with guns in our hands. But whosoever dares to present a serious threat to the Democratic Republic, will be repulsed!

MARTIN: What with?

COUNCILLOR: All bayonets of international reaction will shatter on our unswerving will for peace! (*The THIRD COMRADE laughs him down.*) That's how people look who deny the power of moral persuasion!

FIRST COMRADE: Bleeding heart windbag!

COUNCILLOR: I'm not a windbag! We want to see no more weapons, I myself lost two of my wife's brothers in the war!

FOURTH COMRADE: In the next war it'll be us, me and Stiegler, and him and him!

KRANZ: (*Mimics him.*) And me and me and me!

COUNCILLOR: There isn't going to be another war! We shall know how to prevent such a crime! This I guarantee.

MARTIN: Just like in 1914!

COUNCILLOR: The circumstances were completely different!

STRANGE COMRADE: Always the same, always the same!

COUNCILLOR: And where were you in 1914? In kindergarten!

STRANGE COMRADE: What about you? In 1914 you were boasting about the deeds of your forefathers, that's something our generation certainly can't do!

MARTIN: Comrades! If it goes on like this, one morning soon we'll be waking up in the Holy Roman Empire, Mussolini style!

STRANGE COMRADE: Women comrades and comrades!

KRANZ: (*Beside himself.*) Throw him out, the drunken Prussian lowlife! Out with him! Out!

MARTIN: Quiet! Forget about Prussians! The essential thing is, Italian Nights of this sort need breaking up! Utterly and completely!

COUNCILLOR: Order! Order! By virtue of our statutes I call for the immediate expulsion of Comrade Martin!

ENGELBERT: Bravo!

COUNCILLOR: On the grounds of uncomradely conduct!

MARTIN: Bravo! Let's go! (*Leaves with his COMRADES.*)

COUNCILLOR: We shan't allow a split in our Italian Night, comrades. I've been looking forward to this evening for a fortnight, and I refuse to be split! Music! Sit down!

Scene 6

Outside Josef Lehninger's pub. MARTIN and his COMRADES are emerging from the Italian Night. On the right, a public lavatory.

MARTIN: So, I'm expelled. On the grounds of uncomradely
conduct. You have to laugh.
(*Silence.*)
SECOND COMRADE: Where'll we go?
MARTIN: My place.
STRANGE COMRADE: To work! There isn't a moment
to lose!
MARTIN: The bourgeoisie soon retreats to the landowner's
castle.
STRANGE COMRADE: Be ready!
(*Silence.*)
MARTIN: (*Quietly, mistrustfully.*) Who exactly is he?
FIRST COMRADE: I don't know him.
THIRD COMRADE: He's new to me.
(*They all go into the public lavatory.*)
STRANGE COMRADE: (*Follows them.*) I'm from Magdeburg,
comrades!
MARTIN: (*Voice off. From the lavatory.*) Yes, from Magdeburg.
Which is in Prussia. Well, I simply want to inform you that
I'm the official leader here, and with us it's the custom,
see, that the chosen leader heads the action, not any other
person. Whether he's from Magdeburg or not. (*He reappears
with his COMRADES. Silence.*)
MARTIN: (*To the FIRST COMRADE.*) Is it a fact, then, that
you defaced His Majesty's statue?
SECOND COMRADE: (*Mimics High German.*) We took the
liberty of disfiguring His Majesty's statue with a certain
amount of red colouring matter.
MARTIN: Who's we?
SECOND COMRADE: Me.
FOURTH COMRADE: And me.
MARTIN: So. You as well. That was abysmally stupid of
course. Or don't you think so, gentlemen?
STRANGE COMRADE: Defacing a statue is just a prank,
naturally. Don't waste time with dynasties that have been
thrown out, boys. It's better to ensure that no future statues
get erected to our friends the capitalists!
(*Silence.*)

MARTIN: (*Confers quietly with his COMRADES; then turns to the STRANGE COMRADE.*) I'm going to say something now; in my opinion you're an agent provocateur –

STRANGE COMRADE: (*Horrified.*) Comrade!

MARTIN: So perhaps it's an idea if anyone like that were to take their leave of us, any such strange provocateurs – from Magdeburg. (*Leaves him standing.*)

STRANGE COMRADE: I despair.

MARTIN: Are you still here? I said, are you still here? (*Advances on him menacingly. The STRANGE COMRADE leaves quickly.*)

KARL: (*Comes out of the pub with LENI.*) Everything's chaos in there.

THIRD COMRADE: Glad to hear it!

LENI: Everyone's leaving. The whole atmosphere's gone to hell.

SIXTH COMRADE: Then it's gone where it belongs!

KARL: Martin, I want to ask your forgiveness.

MARTIN: For what?

KARL: For breaking my promise. I know it was cheating, I've thought very hard about that, but in fact it only seemed to be cheating. I only appeared to be breaking it.

MARTIN: What are you trying to tell me?

KARL: Look, I had to dance! I'd actually promised Anna I'd convert the girl here behind me to our way of thinking, and you have to go halfway to meet a girl like her, it only happens bit by bit –

MARTIN: The fact that the only people you ever convert are girls –

KARL: Each to his own. I belong to an older generation than you, it means something, even though there's only five years' difference between us, they're five war years –

MARTIN: Historical forces don't give a toss about private destinies, they stride inexorably over the individual, and always forwards.

KARL: You're absolutely right there.

MARTIN: You'd be useful, if only you could be believed. But that's exactly it, you can't, because you're only half a man.

KARL: You don't have conflicts with your libido. Christ, sometimes I envy you!

MARTIN: I pity you. I've kept on trying with you. Now it's finished. I no longer place any value on your co-operation.

KARL: As you wish! Forgive me! (*Goes off with LENI.*)

(*During this time the COMRADES have also disappeared. ANNA enters.*)

MARTIN: Anna!

ANNA: I'm frightened!

MARTIN: You?

ANNA: I thought you were someone else –

MARTIN: Did you?

ANNA: You were so far away from me just then.

MARTIN: (*Almost scornfully.*) Was I? Did you get anything?

ANNA: Several things.

MARTIN: First?

ANNA: First I discovered the fascists are going to break up our Italian Night –

MARTIN: (*Interrupts her.*) First, it isn't our Italian Night! Second, their Italian Night has already been broken up. I broke it up.

ANNA: So soon?

MARTIN: I'll tell you later! And?

ANNA: The fascists want to beat up everyone here.

MARTIN: Why not. The committee can have that and welcome. Let those creeps experience the results of their treachery on their own heads. We young ones have to leave them to their fate and find our own!

ANNA: I wouldn't do that.

MARTIN: What's this?

ANNA: I wouldn't do it. I'd help them, you know, they're still closer to us than the others.

MARTIN: You don't say!

ANNA: I wouldn't mind if the Councillor got beaten either, but there are other people there in good faith, probably –

MARTIN: (*Scornfully.*) You think so?

ANNA: And anyway it's nothing to do with any third person, the disagreements we have among ourselves! They're our disagreements and that's all!

MARTIN: (*Nastily.*) I take that as your private opinion.

ANNA: Please don't be so patronising.

(*Silence.*)

MARTIN: And?

ANNA: That's all. You know, the fascists are absolutely furious. There's a statue supposed to have been defaced this evening –

MARTIN: Yes, that was that idiot Stiegler –

ANNA: Martin!

MARTIN: (*Surprised.*) What?

ANNA: Martin, if one of us attacked the statue, does that mean the others in there get beaten? I think that's awful! It's not worthy of us! It's immoral –

(*She stops, because MARTIN has suddenly started staring with fascination at her neck. Silence.*)

MARTIN: What's that kind of a mark there?

ANNA: Where?

MARTIN: There.

ANNA: Here? It's a mark –

(*Silence.*)

It'll be a bruise tomorrow.

MARTIN: Well.

ANNA: It's just he was rough.

MARTIN: (*A little unsure.*) So, was he?

ANNA: They all are, men.

(*Silence.*)

MARTIN: Look at me.

(*ANNA doesn't look at him.*)

Why won't you look at me?

ANNA: I can't look at you.

MARTIN: Why can't you look at me? Don't look at me in that stupid way, for heaven's sake!

(*Silence.*)

ANNA: Only just now it seemed so strange to me –

MARTIN: How do you mean?

ANNA: What you asked me to do, I mean to go with some fascist – that it was you who asked me –

MARTIN: What new feelings are these?

ANNA: No, they're old ones –

MARTIN: You know I hate primitive sentimentality.

What's the point of these obsolete problems? Just no illusions, please!

ANNA: Now you're being patronising again.

(*Silence.*)

MARTIN: Anna, so he was rough – our fascist friend.

ANNA: Yes.

MARTIN: How rough?

ANNA: Not specially.

(*Silence.*)

MARTIN: Still he was rough – perhaps it's unworthy of us.

ANNA: What is?

MARTIN: Letting the committee in there get pounded for the sake of his paint-splattered Majesty – by our fascist friends.

ANNA: You see!

MARTIN: What do I see? I see nothing. Nothing! Nothing at all! What I mean is: we won't give the fascists the satisfaction! Come on! (*Leaves with ANNA.*)

(*KARL arrives with LENI. Both seem to be in a bad mood. They sit on a bench by the public lavatory.*)

LENI: Why are you so quiet?

KARL: Because my heart's aching.

LENI: But you can't help it if that Italian Night ended on a bad note!

KARL: Thank you. (*He presses her hand, and then puts his head in his hands.*)

(*Silence.*)

LENI: Your friend Martin reminds me of someone I used to know. There was nothing you could say to him either, because all he really knew about was his motorbike. He won any amount of races, except I disturbed him in his training. Don't be so sad –

KARL: What I'd like right now is not to go on living.

LENI: But why?

KARL: Because my eyes are too sharp. I can see the world's developing and then I think, if only I were a few years younger, I could actively help improve it – but I'm rotten. And tired.

LENI: You're just talking yourself into it.

KARL: Half a man! Only one half cares about anything good, the other half's reactionary.

LENI: Don't be downhearted –

KARL: I think there's a curse on me –

LENI: No, there isn't!

KARL: (*Stands up.*) Yes, there is!
(*Silence.*)

LENI: Do you believe in God?
(*KARL is silent.*)
There is a God, and there's salvation as well.

KARL: I wish I knew who cursed me.

LENI: Let me save you.

KARL: You? Me?

LENI: I've got a thousand Marks, we could start a grocer's shop –

KARL: Us?

LENI: Abroad. With my uncle –

KARL: Us?

LENI: Me and you.
(*Silence.*)

KARL: In cash?

LENI: Yes.
(*Silence.*)

KARL: So what are you thinking? Are you thinking of marriage? No, you're too good for me!

LENI: Oh, you, don't talk so coldly! I know you inside out, even though I've only just met you!
(*Flings herself on him; big kissing scene.*)

KARL: I've actually always dreamed of redemption through woman, but I couldn't believe in it, you see – I'm really very bitter, do you know?

LENI: (*Kisses him on the forehead.*) Yes, it's a wicked world.

Scene 7

In Josef Lehninger's beer garden. The republican Italian Night is now definitely broken up – only the committee is still sitting under the Chinese lanterns, in fact only: The COUNCILLOR with ADELE, BETZ, ENGELBERT, and KRANZ. The latter is snoring with his head on a table. It is nearly midnight, and ADELE is freezing, for there is a cold breeze.

BETZ: What to do, quoth Zeus.

ENGELBERT: Wend our way?

COUNCILLOR: (*Jumps up.*) Never! Not if hell had broken out on earth. We shan't let our Italian Night be destroyed! We stay here, friends, and we don't yield – not till closing time! (*He sits down.*)

ENGELBERT: Hear, hear!

(*The COUNCILLOR nervously lights a cigar.*)

KRANZ: (*Wakes up and yawns wordlessly: to BETZ.*) Listen, I just dreamed something really good.

BETZ: A pleasant dream?

KRANZ: Very. I actually dreamed of a republic, and it was a total republic, even the monarchists were undercover republicans –

BETZ: Obviously it must have been so-called wish-fulfilment.

KRANZ: Hey?

ENGELBERT: Well, then, what about a little game of Tarock?

COUNCILLOR: Tarock?

ENGELBERT: Oats Tarock –

KRANZ: Oats Tarock!

COUNCILLOR: That would certainly be the sensible thing –

ENGELBERT: I've got cards – (*Sits down with the COUNCILLOR and KRANZ under the brightest lantern, shuffles and deals.*) This is a good thought! (*BETZ looks on.*)

COUNCILLOR: First!

ENGELBERT: Second!

KRANZ: Last!

COUNCILLOR: Solo!

KRANZ: 'And the light shineth in darkness' – (*He leads.*) (*Now the wind is stronger.*)

ADELE: (*Gets up and shivers.*) Alfons!

COUNCILLOR: (*Not letting himself be disturbed.*) Yes?

ADELE: When are we going?

COUNCILLOR: I'm not saying it twice! Club!

ADELE: But I'll catch cold –

COUNCILLOR: Sorry, dear. Heart!

KRANZ: And heart!

ENGELBERT: And heart!

BETZ: (*Goes over to ADELE.*) We're staying till closing time, Madam Councillor.

ADELE: When's closing time?

BETZ: Two o'clock.

ADELE: What time is it now?

BETZ: It's just getting on for twelve.

ADELE: Oh God.

COUNCILLOR: (*To BETZ.*) Leave her alone, please!
(*Silence.*)

ADELE: I'll catch my death.

BETZ: Or pneumonia. (*Pause.*) Of course the finest way to die is to die for an ideal.

ADELE: I don't know any ideal I'd like to die for.

BETZ: (*Smiles gently.*) Not even the ideals for which your good husband sacrifices himself?

ADELE: Does he sacrifice himself?

BETZ: Day and night.

ADELE: Well, you'd know.

BETZ: Everything's relative of course.
(*Pause.*)

ADELE: Believe me, a man who hasn't got those sort of public ideals is far nicer to his family. I mean in the strictly human sense. You're an intelligent man, Herr Betz, I can see that.

COUNCILLOR: What are you two talking about so seriously over there?

BETZ: You.

COUNCILLOR: Really? Have you no more interesting topic of conversation?

ADELE: (*Nastily.*) Alfons!

COUNCILLOR: What now?

ADELE: I'd like another ham roll.

COUNCILLOR: You've got through two ham rolls already!
In my view, that should suffice! (*Lights himself another cigar.*)

ADELE: If you can have cigars –

COUNCILLOR: (*Interrupts her.*) You're impossible! Shame on you! Now it won't draw, because you don't allow me anything! (*Furiously throws the cigar away.*) An impossible cigar!

ADELE: (*Gets up.*) I'd like to go home now.
COUNCILLOR: Now don't be difficult, please.
ADELE: I'm going –
COUNCILLOR: I'm staying.
ADELE: Come on!
COUNCILLOR: No. You stay!
ADELE: No, I have to be up again at six o'clock to wash your
    shirts and –
COUNCILLOR: I say you stay!
ADELE: But I'll catch my death here –
COUNCILLOR: You're staying, finito! Understand?
    (*ADELE sits down again with an aggrieved smile.*)
    Play!
ENGELBERT: I'll continue!
KRANZ: Play, as well.
ENGELBERT: Namely?
KRANZ: Grass!
COUNCILLOR: Snails! Beggar! Yes, beggar! And I'll finish
    – (*He quickly wins and laughs resoundingly.*)
    (*Silence.*)
BETZ: Why is it exactly that you don't just go home on your
    own?
ADELE: Because he doesn't let me go on my own.
BETZ: Doesn't let you? He doesn't let you go on your own?
    But he hasn't got any rights over your person. Good heav-
    ens, I'm suddenly seeing him in quite a different light,
    although I half expected it. Alfons Ammetsberger, my old
    fellow warrior – thirty-five years. Yes, yes, it must be age.
    I wonder if I've changed as much.
COUNCILLOR: (*To BETZ.*) Please, Betz, just leave her be!
LANDLORD: (*Appears; he's very drunk and greets them swaying,
    not that anyone takes any notice of him. He grins.*) That's right,
    boycott me, just boycott me! It's all the same to me,
    I won't be crying any tears for you. It has to be said the
    reactionaries are much more obliging customers. Your
    young people only drink lemonade! Some republicans!
    Lemonade! Lemonade!
KRANZ: Shut up!

LANDLORD: (*Suddenly dreamy.*) I'm thinking about my lavatory. You see, originally there was nothing but sex stuff on
the walls in there, then during the war it was all patriotism,
and now it's all politics – believe what I say; until the day
it's all sex again, the German people will never be healthy –
KRANZ: Shut up, you dirty disgusting beast!
LANDLORD: Pardon? Heinrich, you remain the only
reasonable person here, what did that gentleman say?
BETZ: He said you ought to shut up.
LANDLORD: Did he? What a bad chap I am. Apropos;
I've got some delightful news for you, good people.
KRANZ: We're not your good people!
LANDLORD: What did he say?
BETZ: What he said was, we're not your good people.
LANDLORD: Did he say that? Well then, gentlemen!
I have the honour of bringing you a highly gratifying
announcement; namely that you're surrounded,
gentlemen, totally surrounded!
(*The COUNCILLOR listens.*)
BETZ: Who's surrounded?
LANDLORD: You, gentlemen!
ENGELBERT: How's that?
LANDLORD: Gentlemen! To be precise, I've just heard that
the fascist gentlemen are going to give you a pounding –
(*The COUNCILLOR stands up.*) To be precise, the fascist
gentlemen claim you gentlemen defaced the statue –
COUNCILLOR: What statue?
LANDLORD: The statue of His Majesty.
ENGELBERT: I don't know what you're talking about.
LANDLORD: To be precise, the fascist gentlemen have got
fire raging in their bellies and are determined to avenge the
honour of His Majesty! With blood! Hurrah!
KRANZ: Oh you thirty-three-year-old Christ nailed up on high!
LANDLORD: There's absolutely no point in lying, gentlemen!
You're convicted! All the evidence speaks against you!
Cross examination and such!
COUNCILLOR: Lies! Wicked lies! I insist no one here
defaced any statue!

LANDLORD: (*Raises his glass.*) Your very good health!
(*Empties it. Silence.*)

BETZ: Josef, who told you then, that we're supposed to be
beaten up?

LANDLORD: Martin's Anna.

COUNCILLOR: Martin? Interesting!

LANDLORD: Discretion is the better part of valour!

KRANZ: Now I'm totally confused!

ENGELBERT: On the rules of logic, it can only be
a mistake –

COUNCILLOR: (*Sharply.*) Or a betrayal! Our hands are
clean.

LANDLORD: Clean or not – now there'll be whacks,
gentlemen!

KRANZ: You Judas!

LANDLORD: (*Tearfully.*) But I'm not a Judas, gentlemen!
I've always stayed true to you in my soul, even after the
Revolution! But look at the crazy world we're living in!
In the old days a Sunday like this was a sheer delight, and
if there was a bit of a fight for God's sake it was over some
fool of a woman, but never on any account over shit like
politics. These are very worrying symptoms, gentlemen!

KRANZ: I desire to take the floor! I desire to move a motion! I desire to submit that we quietly await the course of
events, secure in the knowledge that we shall be gloriously
vindicated, because after all we are completely innocent!

ENGELBERT: Hear! Hear!

COUNCILLOR: Don't make me laugh!

BETZ: (*To KRANZ.*) Once more you're forgetting man's aggressive drives –

KRANZ: Eh?

LANDLORD: Now there'll be whacks –

BETZ: I'm speaking now from a higher standpoint. Man's
nature is by nature cruel – we must be able to face facts,
dear friend!

LANDLORD: Oh, how true!

COUNCILLOR: Friends! With regard to fate, man is a fragile
reed in the wind, whether he be monarchist or republi-

can. In the end there are moments in life where even the boldest of the voices of reason must bend, albeit against his own feelings! Friends! It would be a poor general indeed who led his brigades into certain defeat. In this spirit I hereby bring our Italian Night to a close! *Vis major, force majeure.* Where's my hat?

BETZ: I'm staying.

COUNCILLOR: What's that?

BETZ: Really I'm of a really somewhat different opinion –

COUNCILLOR: But there should be no different opinion –

BETZ: You think? But in respect of defacing the statue, our conscience is absolutely clear.

ENGELBERT: Quite right!

BETZ: In consequence of which I consider it not right to run away in this fashion.

COUNCILLOR: Not not right, smart! These fascists are known to be greater in number, in consequence of which they're known to be capable of any villainy at any time! Where's my hat?

BETZ: I'm staying. Even if they give me a pounding!
(*Silence.*)

COUNCILLOR: (*Stares at him sarcastically.*) Ah, he's for the politics of catastrophe. Well, I wish you joy of it!

BETZ: Thank you!

COUNCILLOR: (*Grins.*) Good God, how heroic!

BETZ: Better punched around than lily-livered.
(*Silence.*)

COUNCILLOR: You think?

ADELE: I think so too.

COUNCILLOR: There's nothing here for you to think.

ADELE: I still think so.

COUNCILLOR: (*Slowly approaching her, restraining himself.*) There's nothing here for you to think, understand?

ADELE: I'm just saying what's in my mind.

COUNCILLOR: There's nothing here for you to put in your mind.

ADELE: (*Nastily.*) You think?

COUNCILLOR: Don't show me up, you hear?

ADELE: No.
  (*The COUNCILLOR grips her.*)
  Ow! Ow!
COUNCILLOR: Will you pull yourself together?
ADELE: Ow, Alfons! Ow!
COUNCILLOR: Pull yourself together! Pull –
ADELE: (*Breaks away, shrieking.*) Ow! You and your idealism!
COUNCILLOR: Impossible woman!
ADELE: You're impossible! On the outside he's a worker,
  inside he's a capitalist! Your friends here should see what
  you're really like! He knocks me about, me! Thirty years!
  Thirty years! (*She cries.*)
COUNCILLOR: (*With his hand over his eyes.*) Adele! Adele!
  (*Silence. He slowly takes his hand away from his eyes.*) Where's
  my hat?
LANDLORD: (*Gets up with difficulty.*) With or without your
  hat – you are and will remain surrounded –
  (*He belches and staggers off. ADELE suddenly grins.*)
COUNCILLOR: Don't laugh!
ADELE: Looking at you now, it's really funny when I think
  how you've been standing in the way of the young people
  – (*She starts sobbing again.*)
COUNCILLOR: Don't bawl!
ADELE: It's just my nerves –
KRANZ: Typical feminine logic.
ADELE: (*Crying.*) If you hadn't got the young people thrown
  out just now, no one would dare to come in here – now
  we're just a bunch of old cripples –
ENGELBERT: Oho!
COUNCILLOR: God in heaven!
ADELE: Leave God alone!
KRANZ: There is no God.
  (*Silence.*)
  I desire to take the floor! I hereby desire to move a motion!
  I hereby desire to submit that it was, so to speak, rather
  precipitate to expel Martin just like that, as we did, along
  with his following – in fact he has a considerable following,
  a strong following, and not the worst following – and he
  was, so to speak, not entirely in the wrong –

COUNCILLOR: You think?

KRANZ: If we had small-bore rifles now, the same as the fascists, then we wouldn't be having to take a pounding for something we didn't do, instead we could defend ourselves – defend ourselves – that's logical, isn't it?

ENGELBERT: Logical or not! By the statutes Martin was bound to be expelled!

KRANZ: Logical or not! I hereby shit on such statutes!

ENGELBERT: Hear, hear!

KRANZ: The statutes are completely out of date.

COUNCILLOR: Suddenly.

KRANZ: I now desire officially to submit that the precipitate expulsion of our comrade Martin be rendered null and void!

COUNCILLOR: Null and void?

KRANZ: Definitely!

COUNCILLOR: (*Looks around at them enquiringly.*) What's this?

BETZ: Yes!

ENGELBERT: Hm.

COUNCILLOR: (*To ENGELBERT, quietly.*) Yes or no? (*Silence.*)

ENGELBERT: Yes. (*Silence.*)

COUNCILLOR: Where's my hat?

ADELE: (*Passes him his hat.*) Here.

COUNCILLOR: (*Pulls his hat well over his head; tonelessly.*) I shall withdraw from political life – I shan't go out so much – at most play bowls or sing, perhaps –

ADELE: At last, Alfons!

(*Trumpet signal. The MAJOR, in an old colonial uniform, quickly enters the beer garden with two FASCISTS – stops short in front of the COUNCILLOR and stares at him furiously. Silence.*)

MAJOR: I already have the dubious honour of knowing you. (*The COUNCILLOR nods apathetically.*) I see from your wandering looks and from the guilty demeanour of your savoury companions that you have already divined the purpose of my visit.

ENGELBERT: But we're completely innocent!

MAJOR: Silence! Now we have it from your own mouths!
(*Dead silence. He yells.*)
Silence! Summary justice! Red rabble!

BETZ: Everything's relative, you know –

MAJOR: Shut up! By heaven we're going to have done with
you! Vengeance for Strassburg! We'll teach you to go about
damaging monuments – you've attacked our honour, and
blood sticks to our honour!

BETZ: Absolute rubbish!

MAJOR: What! (*BETZ lights a cigar.*) Don't smoke!

BETZ: As you wish –
(*He lays the cigar aside. Silence.*)

MAJOR: Czernowitz!

CZERNOWITZ: Present, Major!

MAJOR: Just tell me, will you – how did your father in the field
treat prisoners of war who attempted passive resistance?

CZERNOWITZ: He had cartridges fired into their backsides
like nails into the wall, Major!

MAJOR: (*To BETZ.*) Understand?

BETZ: (*To CZERNOWITZ, as if teaching a child to speak politely.*)
I don't have a backside – I have a posterior.
(*The MAJOR is walking around the COUNCILLOR;
turns on him suddenly.*)

MAJOR: Hands by your sides! Sit down!
(*The COUNCILLOR sits down as if in a dream. The MAJOR
waves one of the FASCISTS forward. The FASCIST brings the
COUNCILLOR paper, pen and ink.*)
Very well, write what I dictate!
(*The COUNCILLOR obeys apathetically. The MAJOR dictates.*)
I, the red Councillor Alfons Ammetsberger, hereby declare
upon my oath – have you got it – upon my oath – that I
am nothing but a common –
(*The COUNCILLOR stops.*)
Write!
(*The COUNCILLOR starts writing again. The MAJOR dictates.*)
– that I am nothing but a common – mongrel!
(*The COUNCILLOR stops again.*)
Get on with it!

(*The COUNCILLOR doesn't move.*)
If you don't do as you're told, fellow, you'll get it in the backside! Write! Come on!
(*The COUNCILLOR slowly bends over the paper – suddenly starts to whimper and sob.*)

COUNCILLOR: No, but I'm not a –

MAJOR: (*Interrupts him, yelling.*) But you are a mongrel, you're nothing but a common mongrel!

ADELE: You! He isn't a mongrel, you! He's my husband, you! How do you dare, you ridiculous-looking dressed-up creature! Just leave him alone, will you!

BETZ: What on earth right have you to –

MAJOR: (*Interrupts him.*) Shut up!

ADELE: No, you shut up! And take off that rubbish you're wearing, don't you know the war's over, you clown! You should send your pension to the war wounded and find some decent work to do, instead of frightening poor people in their open-air amusements, you common common mongrel!

MAJOR: You vulgar woman! Wait now! Forty German men are standing outside! (*Leaves quickly with his FASCISTS.*)

ADELE: (*Calls after him.*) That's my husband, understand!
(*Great tumult outside the beer garden. MARTIN with ANNA followed by his COMRADES, quickly enter.*)
It's Martin!

MARTIN: At your service, Madam! The air is clear, so to speak, gentlemen! I should confess this visit from our fascist friends was aimed at us, me and my comrades, not at the committee here. And we're made in such a way that we like to answer for what we do. But I think I can say no one here has anything more to fear, because when the fascists saw us they shifted – rapidly. So we've come through again!

COUNCILLOR: Well then! Naturally there's no question of a serious threat to the Democratic Republic. Friends! So long as there exists a Society for the Defence of the Republic, and so long as I have the honour of being chairman of our local branch here, the Republic can sleep soundly!

MARTIN: And good night!

The End.

TALES FROM THE VIENNA WOODS
GESCHICHTEN AUS DEM WIENER WALD
(1931)

'Nothing gives as strong an impression
of infinity as stupidity.'

INTRODUCTION

Christopher Hampton

On June 1, 1938, Ödön von Horváth left his Paris hotel for a meeting with Robert Siodmak, the film producer; they were to discuss the possibility of making a film based on Horváth's novel *Jugend Ohne Gott*. Afterwards, as far as can be established, Horváth went, alone, to a cinema on the Champs Elysées to see Walt Disney's *Snow White and the Seven Dwarfs*. He had made arrangements to meet his friends Hertha Pauli and Carl Frucht that evening in their usual bistro. At about 7.30, he was walking down the Champs Elysées, when a storm of unusual violence arose. He crossed the street and joined a group of people sheltering under a chestnut tree opposite the Théâtre Marigny. As the storm continued, an adjacent elm collapsed on to the chestnut tree, causing a branch to break off. It struck Horváth on the back of the head, killing him instantly. No one else was hurt. He was the author of seventeen plays (not counting sketches, fragments and rewrites), three novels and other miscellaneous pieces. He was 36.

It was in 1931 that Horváth, at any rate in terms of critical success and public recognition, reached the peak of his career. In that year he was awarded the Kleist prize, then the most prestigious of German literary awards, by Carl Zuckmayer, himself, along with Brecht and Robert Musil, a former winner of the prize. The Nazi press was incensed by the spectacle of Zuckmayer ('the half-Jew') awarding a German prize to Horváth ('the young Hungarian'): as well it might have been since Horváth's play *Italienishe Nacht* (Italian Night) had attacked and derided the Nazis even more mercilessly than Zuckmayer's *Captain of Köpenich*. 'The German proposes and the Jew disposes,' the *Völkischer Beobachter* declared mysteriously in the course of a typically frenzied attack on the award.

And it was in 1931, in November, that Horváth's play *Geschichten aus dem Wiener Wald* (Tales from the Vienna Woods) had its première at the Deutsches Theater, Berlin, directed by Heinz Hilpert, with Peter Lorre as Alfred and Carola Neher as

Marianne. It was an immediate success and has remained the most popular and often-performed of his plays; but even so, the minority who booed and hissed at the first night were a reminder of how fragile was the position in which at that time the most talented German writers found themselves.

His father was a Hungarian diplomat and his childhood was spent in the various cities in which his father was posted. He was fourteen, he said, before he wrote a sentence in German. Nevertheless, he thought of himself, and felt it necessary, in those racially-conscious times, to stress this in interviews, as a German writer, although he retained his Hungarian passport. 'I'm a typically Austro-Hungarian affair,' he said.

Tales from the Vienna Woods, like *Italian Night,* which preceded it, and *Kasimir und Karoline,* which followed, was described by Horváth as a *Volksstück,* a term it would not be particularly meaningful to translate, as, essentially, it was a critical renovation of a tradition we are not familiar with, that of the nineteenth-century Austrian comedies of Nestroy and Raimund. In fact these three plays, generally regarded as Horváth's masterpieces, evolved a style as personal to Horváth as so-called 'epic theatre' was to Brecht. 'More a descriptive form than a dramatic form', Horváth said, and his purpose was nothing less than to describe, in large-scale, but carefully constructed plays, the decay of a society haunted by inflation (an earlier play, Sladek, was subtitled 'a history from the age of inflation') and lurching towards Fascism. Horváth, unlike Brecht, was not a didactic writer, asking on the one hand for a cool, detached audience and on the other hand presenting them with an open-and-shut case; and indeed, if you look at the earlier drafts and scenes eventually not included in *Tales from the Vienna Woods,* it is clear that Horváth drew back from anything that might seem too crudely oversimplified. The interplay between individual selfishness and the pressures of a society in crisis is impartially portrayed, and only the liveliness and compassion with which each individual character, even the most reprehensible, is drawn, show where Horváth's sympathies lay. All these plays deal with losers in what Horváth called 'the gigantic battle between the individual and society' and behind them lies a powerful sense of people who have been through bad times and have still worse to come.

Worse came. Horváth's next play *Glaube Liebe Hoffnung* (Faith, Hope and Charity), a more intimate, small-scale piece than the preceding three plays, went into rehearsal in 1933. It never opened. Shortly afterwards, his parents' house in Murnau was ransacked by the SA, and Horváth set off into the half-life of exile. For the next five years he travelled almost continuously, sometimes venturing back into Germany, while his newest plays remained either unperformed or received matinée performances in Vienna or German-language performances in Prague. His work became harsher and darker and he ventured into new areas with two plays which used familiar figures as a means to examine the themes of exile and the breakdown of society, *Figaro Läßt Sich Scheiden* (Figaro Gets a Divorce) and *Don Juan Kommt Aus Dem Krieg* (Don Juan Comes Back From the War), the latter perhaps the strongest and most despairing play he wrote. Finally, whether exasperated by the pointlessness of writing plays which were unlikely to be satisfactorily performed, or gripped by a new inspiration, he turned back to the novel, a form he had used only once before. The result was *Jugend Ohne Gott* (Youth Without God), a brilliant study of the *Hitlerjugend*, which was an immediate success and was translated into several languages. He followed this up with *Ein Kind Unserer Zeit* (A Child of our Time), working frenziedly now, and announcing, soon after it was finished, that he was going to start on another novel, *Adieu Europa*. He left Vienna on 13 March, 1938, just in time, as it turned out, and the next two months, as his exile began in earnest, were like some speeded-up parody of his childhood: Prague, Budapest, Trieste, Venice, Milan, Zurich, Brussels and Amsterdam. Eventually, on 28 May, he arrived in Paris.

After Horváth's bizarre and sensational death, his name passed into obscurity for about twenty years. Then, towards the end of the fifties, his plays gradually began to reappear in the repertoire of German theatre, and what came to be known as the 'Horváth Renaissance' slowly gathered momentum, until, in the 1970-71 season, there were twenty-five major productions of Horváth's plays in German-speaking theatres. Even more significantly, a number of young playwrights, including Franz Xaver Kroetz, Martin Sperr and Wolfgang Bauer, declared their allegiance to Horváth, and he replaced Brecht as the central influence on new German and Austrian plays. Peter Handke, as well, writing in 1968 on Horváth, took the opportunity to launch a broadside against Brecht, contrasting his simple solutions 'which for me are nothing more than a *bon mot* or an aphorism', with the much richer texture and far more ambiguous effects of Horváth, who has the ability, 'elsewhere only to be found in Chekhov or Shakespeare', to write a line, often banal in itself, but so dislocating, as to suggest and contain an infinite variety of response.

When I began work on this translation, I received a number of amiable messages, more or less implying that the project was impossible. Horváth's use of language was so personal, *Tales from the Vienna Woods* so local in its atmosphere, that any attempt to convey the flavour of the play in English was unlikely to succeed. The fact that none of Horváth's plays (with the curious exception of *Sladek*, broadcast on Radio 3 in 1970) have been performed in English, to my knowledge, was not simply a reflection of the notorious insularity of the English-speaking theatre; there were other reasons, to wit, the man's work was simply untranslatable. To begin with, there was the problem of the dialect. Then there was Horváth's individual use of the dialect. And so on.

All this is true: and this, although it is as accurate as I can make it, does not pretend to be a scholarly translation of the play. I have not attempted to find an equivalent English dialect, because in England (as is not the case in Vienna) dialect is inextricably connected with class, and the result would have been inevitably misleading. I was fortified in this decision by Horváth's own remarks in his *Gebrauchsanweisung* (Instructions), written reluctantly as a result of his dissatisfaction with a number of productions of his plays. In the course of this document he lists a number of directors' deadly sins, the first of which starts as follows: '1. Dialect. Not a word to be spoken in dialect! Every word must be spoken in good German (*hochdeutsch*), at any rate as if spoken by someone who normally only speaks in dialect, and is now forcing himself to speak good German. This is very important!' I have therefore chosen a neutral language, differentiated of course, from character to character, but flexible enough, I hope, to conform to Horváth's enigmatic (and occasionally contradictory) instructions.

Sean O'Casey would have been a wonderful translator of Horváth: and an Irish writer might well have been able to provide a more colourful version of some of Horváth's more eccentric turns of phrase than I have managed. But this is only a beginning for a great and original writer, who has much to say to us, that is both narrowly relevant (and I write on a day when the pound has fallen seven cents against the dollar) and perennially true.

I should like to thank Ian Huish and Maximilian Schell, who have both worked patiently through the text with me, pointing out errors and making valuable suggestions. Their purpose throughout was to bring me closer to Horváth, and any distance that still remains is my fault, not theirs.

In 1971, an indignant reader wrote to the *Rheinische Post* to complain about the misleading title of *Tales from the Vienna Woods*. This deliberate irony on Horváth's part, this violent contrast between the cliché Vienna (Strauss waltzes and old imperial bonhomie) and the stark and bitter reality had deceived and enraged him. The letter ended: 'No one should blame Johann Strauss. He was not in a position to protect his title. His waltzes travelled all over the world. Horváth's miserable series of everyday episodes will scarcely achieve that.'

I believe it will.

Horváth was a deeply superstitious man: and in a time when fear at what was happening in Europe was widespread among intellectuals, Horváth suffered from a number of more (apparently) irrational fears. 'There are worse things than the Nazis,' he once said, 'for example, the things one is afraid of without knowing why.'

In Amsterdam, the week before his death, Horváth visited a clairvoyant (male or female, accounts differ). In any event, the clairvoyant became extremely excited and told him that he must go to Paris, it was absolutely essential, because the greatest adventure of his life awaited him there. As we know, he took the advice.

Almost exactly a year before his death, Horváth was talking to his friend Franz Theodor Csokor, explaining to him why he, Horváth, tried never to go out at the end of May or the beginning of June, because of his conviction that he would die an accidental death on one of those dates. In the course of that conversation, he said something which, apart from its uncanny prophetic quality, seems to me to illuminate the strange atmosphere which clings to even the most ordinary exchanges in *Tales From the Vienna Woods*. He said: 'Why is it most people are afraid of the darkness of the forest? Why aren't they afraid of walking down the street?'

Christopher Hampton, 1977

Characters

ALFRED
MOTHER
GRANDMOTHER
FERDINAND VON HIERLINGER
VALERIE
OSKAR
IDA
HAVLITSCHEK
THE CAPTAIN
THE LADY
MARIANNE
ZAUBERKÖNIG
FIRST AUNT
SECOND AUNT
ERICH
EMMA
HELENE
THE SERVANT
THE BARONESS
THE CONFESSOR
THE AMERICAN
THE COMPÈRE

The action of the play takes place in 1931, in Vienna, in the Vienna Woods and in the Wachau region outside Vienna.

English translations of the songs in the text appear at the end of the book.

This translation of *Tales From The Vienna Woods* was first performed at the Olivier Theatre (Royal National Theatre) on 26 January 1977 with the following cast:

ALFRED, Stephen Rea

MOTHER, Susan Williamson

GRANDMOTHER, Madoline Thomas

FERDINAND VON HIERLINGER, Oliver Cotton

VALERIE, Elizabeth Spriggs

OSKAR, Warren Clarke

IDA, Rowena Shah

HAVLITSCHEK, Pitt Wilkinson

THE CAPTAIN, Nicholas Selby

THE LADY, Vivienne Burgess

MARIANNE, Kate Nelligan

ZAUBERKÖNIG, Paul Rogers

FIRST AUNT, Rosamund Greenwood

SECOND AUNT, Ann Way

ERICH, Struan Rodger

EMMA, Toyah Wilcox

HELENE, Sylvia Coleridge

THE SERVANT, Anne Leon

THE BARONESS, Ellen Pollock

THE CONFESSOR, John Gill

THE AMERICAN, Peter Carlisle

THE COMPÈRE, Trevor Ray

Director, Maximilian Schell

Designers, Timothy O'Brien and Tazeena Firth

Lighting, David Hersey

Music arragement, Robert Stewart

Choreography, Peter Walker

Stage Manager, John Rothenberg

ACT ONE

Scene 1

Out in the Wachau

The entrance to a cottage at the foot of a ruined castle. ALFRED sits in the open air, tucking into bread and butter and curds. His MOTHER is just bringing him a sharper knife. There's a humming and ringing in the air, as if the dying strains of Johann Strauss's waltz 'Tales from the Vienna Woods' were being played somewhere over and over again. And the beautiful blue Danube is not far off. Alfred's MOTHER watches him. Suddenly she grips his hand, the one holding the knife, and looks deep into his eyes. ALFRED, startled, stares at her suspiciously, his mouth full of food. Silence. She strokes his hair, slowly.

MOTHER: It's sweet of you, Alfred dear… I'm so glad you haven't completely forgotten your poor old mother, dear…

ALFRED: What do you mean, completely forgotten you? I would've come out ages ago, if I could've managed it. But nowadays, what with the depression and everyone rushing about, you can't get anything done. If my friend Ferdinand von Hierlinger hadn't brought me out in his convertible, who's to say when you'd've seen me.

MOTHER: I'm sure it's very thoughtful of your friend, Herr von Hierlinger.

ALFRED: Yes, well, he's kindness itself. He's coming to fetch me in half an hour or so.

MOTHER: Already?

ALFRED: Afraid so.

MOTHER: Don't eat all the curds then, otherwise I'll have nothing to offer him…

ALFRED: He doesn't want curds, Hierlinger, he's not allowed them anyway, he's got chronic nicotine poisoning. He's a proper businessman, very well thought of. I see a great deal of him.

MOTHER: On business?

ALFRED: Among other things.

(*Silence.*)

MOTHER: Are you still with the bank?

ALFRED: No.

MOTHER: Why not?

(*Silence.*)

ALFRED: The bank's no use to me, you got no opportunities, it's a dead end. Work in the old sense, it's just not worth the candle. Nowadays, if you want to get on, what you have to do is use other people's work. I'm on my own now. Handling money, that kind of thing…

(*He chokes and coughs violently. His MOTHER slaps him on the back.*)

MOTHER: Isn't it nice?

ALFRED: Yes, but I practically choked.

MOTHER: I'm glad it's nice, anyway.

(*Silence.*)

ALFRED: Speaking of choking, where's Granny?

MOTHER: I think she's in the kitchen, praying.

ALFRED: Praying?

MOTHER: Well, she's been worrying a lot lately.

ALFRED: Worrying?

(*Silence.*)

MOTHER: Don't forget her birthday, whatever you do. She's eighty next month, and if you forget her birthday, we'll have hell again. You are her favourite, you know.

ALFRED: I'll make a note of it. (*He makes a note of it.*) Granny's birthday. Eighty. (*He gets up, full.*) What you might call a biblical age. (*He looks at his watch.*) Nearly time for Hierlinger, I think. He should be here any minute. He'll have a lady with him.

MOTHER: What sort of a lady?

ALFRED: Oldish.

(*Silence.*)

MOTHER: How old?

ALFRED: Middle-aged, you know.

MOTHER: Rich?

ALFRED: How should I know?

(*Silence.*)

MOTHER: Nothing wrong with money. It's just you've never found the right girl.

ALFRED: Maybe. Sometimes I think I'd like to have a few kids around me, but then I think, well, if it's not to be…

(*Alfred's GRANDMOTHER comes out of the cottage, carrying her bowl of curds.*)

GRANDMOTHER: Frieda! Frieda!

MOTHER: Where's the fire?

GRANDMOTHER: Who's stolen my curds?

MOTHER: Me. Our Alfred was still hungry.

(*Silence.*)

GRANDMOTHER: Oh, he was, was he? Nobody bothers to ask me. I might just as well be dead. (*To MOTHER.*) That'd suit you, wouldn't it?

(*ALFRED sticks his tongue out at her.*)

ALFRED: Yah!

(*Silence. Then she sticks her tongue out at ALFRED.*)

GRANDMOTHER: Yah!

(*Silence.*)

(*Shrieking.*) I don't want it anyway! So there!

(*She throws away the contents of the bowl. FERDINAND VON HIERLINGER enters with VALERIE, carefully made-up, fiftyish, wearing a motoring outfit.*)

ALFRED: May I introduce you? This is my mother and this is my friend Ferdinand Hierlinger. Frau Valerie…and over there is my dear old granny.

MOTHER: It's very kind of you, Herr von Hierlinger, to bring Alfred out to see me, thank you, thank you very much…

HIERLINGER: Oh, please, it's nothing. Alfred knows I'll be only too happy to bring him out here whenever he likes, he only has to say the word.

MOTHER: Does he?

HIERLINGER: Of course…

(*He stops, realising he has somehow blundered. Embarrassed silence.*)

VALERIE: It's so beautiful out here…

MOTHER: Perhaps they'd like to have a look round the tower?

HIERLINGER: What tower?

MOTHER: Ours. Up there.

HIERLINGER: You mean to say those lovely romantic ruins are yours?

MOTHER: No, they belong to the state. We just look after them. But I'd be delighted to show you round if you like. If you climb up to the top you'll be rewarded with a magnificent view and a most instructive panorama.

HIERLINGER: Too kind, dear lady, I'd love to, love to.

MOTHER: (*Smiling, embarrassed.*) It'll be a pleasure.
(*To VALERIE.*) And perhaps you'd erm…

VALERIE: No, no thanks, I'm so sorry, but the height, you know, I can never get my breath.

MOTHER: Well, we shan't be long.
(*She exits with HIERLINGER.*)

VALERIE: (*To ALFRED.*) Would you mind just helping me out on a point of information?

ALFRED: What's your problem?
(*GRANDMOTHER sits at the table, tries unsuccessfully to eavesdrop.*)

VALERIE: You've been cheating me again.

ALFRED: Will that be all?

VALERIE: Hierlinger tells me the pay-out on the last race at Saint-Cloud was not a hundred and sixty-eight schillings, it was two hundred and twenty-two schillings.

ALFRED: Hierlinger's lying.

VALERIE: And the paper, I suppose that's lying too?
(*She waves a racing newspaper under his nose. Silence.*)
(*Triumphantly.*) Well?

ALFRED: You're not a fair woman, do you know that? This kind of thing, you're just driving me away from you.

VALERIE: Now perhaps you'll be so kind as to pay me what you owe me. Twenty-seven schillings. *S'il vous plaît.*
(*ALFRED gives her the money.*)

ALFRED: *Voilà!*

VALERIE: *Merci.*
(*She counts it.*)

ALFRED: You are a mean-minded individual.

VALERIE: I am not an individual. And from now on I shall
have to insist on a written receipt, whenever you…

ALFRED: (*Interrupting her.*) Oh, do stop rabbitting on,
will you?
(*Silence.*)

VALERIE: I wish you wouldn't cheat me all the time,
Alfred…

ALFRED: And I wish you wouldn't be so suspicious all the
time, it's just ruining our arrangement. You have to take
into account the fact there's light and shade in any young
man, it's only natural. And just one word in your ear:
any personal relationship, the only thing makes it work is
when there's something in it for both of you. All the rest is
rubbish. So, you're right, there's no reason to break off a
friendly business relationship, just because the other's not
doing us any good…

VALERIE: (*Interrupting him.*) I never said that, I…

ALFRED: There you go, you see, changing your tune again.
You're very frivolous, you know, you really are, not to
mention arrogant. I take a Civil Service widow's pension
and what do I do with it? I use a bit of nous, I know a bit
about horses, and because of my lucky touch, instead of a
Civil Service widow's pension, you're drawing the same
salary as the full-time head of some government department. Now what's the matter?

VALERIE: I was just thinking about the grave.

ALFRED: What grave?

VALERIE: His grave. I can't help it, whenever I hear the
words Civil Service, I think about his grave. (*Pause.*) I don't
do nearly enough to look after it. My God, I should think
it's all overgrown…

ALFRED: Listen, Valerie, if I win tomorrow at Maisons-Laffitte,
we'll have his grave completely overhauled. We'll go halves.
(*VALERIE suddenly kisses his hand.*)
Get off…

HIERLINGER: (*Off.*) Alfred! Alfred! It's beautiful up here.
I'm on my way down.

ALFRED: (*Calling up to him.*) Ready! (*He stares at VALERIE.*)
Are you crying?

VALERIE: (*Tearfully.*) Of course not... (*She looks at herself in her mirror.*) God, I'm a mess...time I shaved again. (*She puts on same more lipstick and hums Chopin's 'Funeral March'.*)

GRANDMOTHER: Alfred!

(*ALFRED goes over to her.*) When are you coming again? Soon?

ALFRED: Sure.

GRANDMOTHER: I don't like goodbyes, you know. As long as nothing happens to you, I can't help worrying...

ALFRED: What's going to happen to me?

(*Silence.*)

GRANDMOTHER: When am I going to get my money back?

ALFRED: Soon as I have it.

GRANDMOTHER: Thing is, I need it.

ALFRED: What do you need money for?

GRANDMOTHER: I'm eighty next month, and when I'm buried, I want it paid for with my own money, I don't want charity, you know what I'm like...

ALFRED: Don't you worry about it, Granny.

Scene 2

Quiet street in Vienna 8

From left to right: OSKAR's superior butcher's shop, with sides of beef and veal, sausages, hams and boars' heads on display. Next to it a dolls' hospital, under the sign 'Zum Zauberkönig', with jokes and novelties, death's heads, dolls, toys, tin soldiers and a skeleton in the window. Finally, a small tobacconist's with newspapers, periodicals and picture postcards in front of the door. Above the dolls' hospital, a balcony with flowers, part of the ZAUBERKÖNIG's flat.

OSKAR stands in the doorway of his shop in his white apron, cleaning his fingernails with a penknife. Every now and then he stops to listen, for on the second floor someone is playing 'Tales from the Vienna Woods' by Johann Strauss on a clapped-out piano.

IDA, a bright, thin, short-sighted eleven-year-old, comes out of the butcher's with her shopping-bag, and is on the way out, right, when she stops in front of the dolls' hospital and looks in the window.

HAVLITSCHEK, OSKAR's assistant, a huge man with bloody hands and an equally bloody apron, appears in the doorway of the butcher's. He is devouring a sausage and he's furious.

HAVLITSCHEK: Stupid bitch, stupid...

OSKAR: Who?

　　(*HAVLITSCHEK points at IDA with his long knife.*)

HAVLITSCHEK: That one. Told me my blood-sausage was off, didn't she, stupid little bitch. My God, for two pins I'd stick her and watch her running round with the knife in her throat, like that pig yesterday, that'd be a laugh.

OSKAR: (*Smiles.*) You think so?

　　(*IDA senses OSKAR's gaze, and it frightens her. All of a sudden she runs off, right. HAVLITSCHEK laughs. The CAPTAIN enters, left. He's been pensioned off since the end of the war, and is in civilian clothes. He nods to OSKAR. OSKAR and HAVLITSCHEK bow: and the waltz comes to an end.*)

CAPTAIN: Well, I really must say, that blood-sausage yesterday. My compliments. First class.

OSKAR: Tender, wasn't it?

CAPTAIN: A poem.

OSKAR: Hear that, Havlitschek?

CAPTAIN: Oh, is he the one we have to...?

HAVLITSCHEK: Ready for inspection, Captain.

CAPTAIN: My respects.

HAVLITSCHEK: You're a real connoisseur, Captain, sir. A gourmand. A man of the world.

CAPTAIN: (*To OSKAR.*) I've been transferred to just about every corner of our old monarchy in my time, but what I always say is, standards. That's what counts. Standards.

OSKAR: It's all a question of tradition, Captain.

CAPTAIN: If your poor dear mother had been spared, she'd have been very proud of her son.

OSKAR: (*Smiles, flattered.*) Well, it just wasn't to be, Captain.

CAPTAIN: Yes, we all have to go some time.

OSKAR: She's been gone a year today.

CAPTAIN: Who?

OSKAR: My mama. After lunch, about half past two.
That's when Our Lord released her from her troubles.
(*Silence.*)

CAPTAIN: Is it a year already?
(*Silence.*)

OSKAR: If you'll excuse me, Captain, I have to go and get
spruced up. For the requiem mass.
(*He exits. No reaction from the CAPTAIN, who is
elsewhere. Silence.*)

CAPTAIN: Another year gone. Pace till twenty, trot till forty,
and then comes the gallop.
(*Silence.*)

HAVLITSCHEK: (*Eating again.*) Beautiful funeral they give
the old lady.

CAPTAIN: Yes, it was a great success.
(*He leaves him standing there and crosses to the
tobacconist's, pausing for a moment to look at the skeleton
in the window of the dolls' hospital. Upstairs, someone
starts playing again, this time the waltz 'Über den Wellen'.
HAVLITSCHEK watches the CAPTAIN's progress, then
spits out the sausage-skin and goes back into the butcher's.
VALERIE appears in the doorway of her tobacconist's.
The CAPTAIN greets her and she responds.*)
May I have a look at the lottery results?
(*VALERIE gets them from the rack by the door and hands
them to him.*)
Enchanté.
(*He buries himself in the list of results. The waltz suddenly
breaks off, in mid-phrase.*)

VALERIE: (*Maliciously.*) And what have we won, then,
Captain? The big prize?
(*The CAPTAIN hands her back the list.*)

CAPTAIN: I've never yet won anything, Frau Valerie.
Goodness knows why the devil I bother. The most I've
ever managed is to win my stake back.

VALERIE: Well, lucky in love…

CAPTAIN: Long ago, long ago.

VALERIE: Come on, Captain, with your profile?

CAPTAIN: If you're a choosy sort of a chap, I'm afraid that has very little to do with it. And it can be expensive, if your character's that way inclined. If the war had only lasted a fortnight longer, I'd be drawing a major's pension today.

VALERIE: If the war had lasted a fortnight longer, we'd have won.

CAPTAIN: As far as one can tell.

VALERIE: There's no doubt about it.

(She exits into her shop. MARIANNE shows a LADY out of the dolls' hospital. Every time the shop door opens, there's a peal of bells. The CAPTAIN leafs through a newspaper and eavesdrops.)

LADY: I can rely on you, then, can I?

MARIANNE: Absolutely, madam. This is the best and oldest shop in the whole district. And we specialise in tin soldiers. They're guaranteed and we always deliver on time.

LADY: I'll go over it again, shall I, just to make sure everything's clear. That's three boxes of seriously wounded and two boxes of dead. And cavalry as well, please, not just infantry. And you will be sure to deliver them early the day after tomorrow, otherwise there'll be tears from the little one. It's his birthday on Friday, and he's been wanting to play doctor for ages…

MARIANNE: They're guaranteed and we always deliver on time, madam. Thank you very much, madam.

LADY: Well, goodbye then.

(She exits, left. The ZAUBERKÖNIG appears on his balcony in his dressing-gown. His moustaches are still taped.)

ZAUBERKÖNIG: Marianne? Where are you?

MARIANNE: Papa?

ZAUBERKÖNIG: Where have you hidden my suspenders?

MARIANNE: The pink ones or the beige ones?

ZAUBERKÖNIG: There's only the pink ones left.

MARIANNE: They're in your chest of drawers, top left-hand drawer, right-hand side at the back.

ZAUBERKÖNIG: Top left-hand drawer, right-hand side at the back. *Difficile est, satiram non scribere.*
(*He disappears.*)

CAPTAIN: (*To MARIANNE.*) Always on the go, Fräulein Marianne. Always on the go.

MARIANNE: Nothing wrong with hard work, Captain.

CAPTAIN: Far from it. By the way, when will our congratulations be in order?

MARIANNE: What for?

CAPTAIN: Well, your engagement.
(*The ZAUBERKÖNIG reappears on the balcony.*)

ZAUBERKÖNIG: Marianne!

CAPTAIN: Good morning to you, Herr Zauberkönig.

ZAUBERKÖNIG: Good morning to you, Captain. Look, Marianne, for the last time, where are my suspenders?

MARIANNE: Where they always are.

ZAUBERKÖNIG: Now what sort of an answer is that, I ask you? And a very nice tone of voice, I must say. Is that the way to speak to your father? Wherever it is they always are, they aren't there.

MARIANNE: Then they're in the cupboard.

ZAUBERKÖNIG: No.

MARIANNE: Then they're in your bedside cabinet.

ZAUBERKÖNIG: No.

MARIANNE: Then they're in with your underpants.

ZAUBERKÖNIG: No.

MARIANNE: Then I don't know where they are.

ZAUBERKÖNIG: I'm asking you once and for all: where are my suspenders?

MARIANNE: I don't know, I'm not a magician!

ZAUBERKÖNIG: (*Yells at her.*) And I'm not going to the requiem mass with my socks round my ankles! Just because you're sloppy with my clothes! Now come up here and look for them! Come on, *avanti, avanti!*
(*MARIANNE exits into the dolls' hospital. As she does so, the waltz 'Über den Wellen' starts up again. The ZAUBERKÖNIG listens.*)

CAPTAIN: Who's that playing?

ZAUBERKÖNIG: She's a schoolgirl. Lives on the second floor. Talented child, she is.

CAPTAIN: Musical.

ZAUBERKÖNIG: Precocious.

(*He hums the tune, sniffs the flowers, enjoying their scent.*)

CAPTAIN: Spring soon, Herr Zauberkönig.

ZAUBERKÖNIG: It's taken long enough! Even the weather's gone mad.

CAPTAIN: Like everyone else.

ZAUBERKÖNIG: Not me. (*Pause.*) It's a miserable time though, Captain, miserable. You can't even afford a servant any more. If I didn't have my daughter...

(*OSKAR comes out of the butcher's, dressed in black and wearing a top hat. He is pulling on a pair of black kid gloves.*)

I shan't keep you a minute, Oskar. It's Marianne. She's lost my suspenders again, thanks to her magic touch.

CAPTAIN: Perhaps you'll permit me to offer you my suspenders, Herr Zauberkönig. I've taken to wearing garters as well, this last...

ZAUBERKÖNIG: How very kind of you, *enchanté*, but we must have order. Marianne will just have to use her magic touch to find them again.

CAPTAIN: May I congratulate the prospective bridegroom?

(*OSKAR lifts his hat and bows slightly.*)

ZAUBERKÖNIG: God willing.

CAPTAIN: Good day, gentlemen.

(*He exits, and the waltz ends. MARIANNE steps on to the balcony with the pink suspenders.*)

MARIANNE: Here we are, I've found your suspenders.

ZAUBERKÖNIG: About time.

MARIANNE: You threw them in the linen basket by mistake. I had to go poking through all the dirty washing.

ZAUBERKÖNIG: Well well well. (*He smiles paternally and pinches her cheek.*) Clever girl. Oskar's down there.

(*He exits.*)

OSKAR: Marianne! Marianne!

MARIANNE: Yes?

OSKAR: Aren't you coming down?

MARIANNE: I've got to anyway.

(*She exits. HAVLITSCHEK appears in the doorway of the butcher's, eating again.*)

HAVLITSCHEK: I wanted to ask you, Herr Oskar. Say an Our Father for me, will you, please, for your poor old mother?

OSKAR: I'd he glad to, Havlitschek.

HAVLITSCHEK: Thanks.

(*He exits. MARIANNE comes out of the dolls' hospital.*)

OSKAR: I'm very happy, Marianne. It's almost over now, my year of mourning, and tomorrow I won't have to wear my crape any more. And the engagement's announced on Sunday, and we'll get married at Christmas. Give us a kiss, Marianne, just a little good morning kiss.

(*MARIANNE kisses him, then pulls away suddenly.*)

MARIANNE: Ow! Why d'you always have to bite?

OSKAR: Did I?

MARIANNE: Don't you even know when you're doing it?

OSKAR: I could have sworn...

MARIANNE: Why d'you always have to hurt me?

(*Silence.*)

OSKAR: Cross?

(*Silence.*)

Are you?

MARIANNE: Sometimes I think what you really want in your heart of hearts is for me to behave really badly.

OSKAR: Marianne! You know how religious I am. I take my Christian principles very seriously

MARIANNE: I suppose you think I'm an atheist, do you? Huh!

OSKAR: I didn't mean to insult you. I know you despise me.

MARIANNE: You are an idiot, what are you talking about?

(*Silence.*)

OSKAR: Don't you love me, then?

MARIANNE: Love, what is it?

(*Silence.*)

OSKAR: What are you thinking about?

MARIANNE: Oskar, if there's anyone going to make us split up, it's you. You mustn't keep pestering me about what I'm thinking, please…

OSKAR: I wish I could see inside your head. I wish I could get inside your skull and find out what you're thinking in there.

MARIANNE: Well, you can't.

OSKAR: Man is an island.

(*Silence. OSKAR fetches a bag of sweets out of his pocket.*) Would you like a sweet, I forgot I had them, the ones in gold paper are liqueur.

(*MARIANNE sticks a large sweet in her mouth, mechanically. The ZAUBERKÖNIG hurries out of his shop, also wearing black and a top hat.*)

ZAUBERKÖNIG: Well, here we are then. What's that you've got there? Sweets again? Well, that's very kind, very kind indeed. (*He puts one in his mouth.*) Pineapple! Delicious! Well, what have you got to say to your fiancé, then? Happy?

(*MARIANNE exits quickly into the dolls' hospital.*)

(*Surprised.*) What's the matter with her, then?

OSKAR: Bad mood.

ZAUBERKÖNIG: Sauce! She doesn't know when she's well off.

OSKAR: Come on, it's getting late, Papa, the mass…

ZAUBERKÖNIG: That's no way to behave. I hope you're not spoiling her. Don't do that, Oskar, whatever you do. You'll suffer for it if you do. What do you think I had to put up with in my marriage? And not because my lady wife was a bad-tempered old hag, God bless her, but because I could never bring myself to do anything dishonourable. Never let go of your authority. Keep your distance. Remember, it's a patriarchy, not a matriarchy. So, chin up and thumbs down! *Ave Caesar, morituri te salutant!*

(*He exits with OSKAR. Upstairs, the schoolgirl starts playing Ziehrer's waltz 'In Lauschiger Nacht'.*
MARIANNE appears in the window, re-arranging the display. She takes particular trouble with the skeleton.)

ALFRED enters, left, catches sight of MARIANNE's back, stops and watches her. MARIANNE turns, sees ALFRED and looks at him with some fascination. ALFRED smiles. MARIANNE smiles back. ALFRED bows, charmingly. MARIANNE acknowledges him. ALFRED approaches the window. VALERIE is standing in the doorway of her shop watching ALFRED. ALFRED drums on the window. MARIANNE looks at him, suddenly frightened, and pulls the blind down quickly. The waltz breaks off, in mid-phrase. ALFRED notices VALERIE. Silence.)

VALERIE: And where are you off to?

ALFRED: To see you, darling.

VALERIE: Lost something, have we?

ALFRED: I thought I might buy you a dolly.

VALERIE: And to think I pinned all my hopes on a creature like you.

ALFRED: Sorry, I'm sure.

(Silence. ALFRED chucks VALERIE under the chin. VALERIE slaps his hand. Silence.)

Who's that girl, then?

VALERIE: None of your bloody business.

ALFRED: Very pretty girl, is that.

VALERIE: Ha!

ALFRED: Fine figure of a girl. How come I've never seen her before? That's what I call a cruel twist of fate.

VALERIE: Do you?

ALFRED: Now, listen, you, I'm not going to put up with your hysterical jealousy much longer. I don't let anyone push me around, that's something I can very well do without.

VALERIE: Oh, can you?

ALFRED: And don't think I give a damn about your money.

(Silence.)

VALERIE: Yes, that would be best, I think…

ALFRED: What would?

VALERIE: It would be best not to see each other any more.

ALFRED: Well, about bloody time! I should think so. I've been waiting for that. There you are. That's what I owe you. With your receipt. We broke even at Saint-Cloud and we won at Le Tremblay. Outsiders. You'd better check it!

(*He exits. VALERIE, alone, counts the money mechanically. Then, a lingering look after ALFRED.*)
VALERIE: (*Quietly.*) Bastard. Shit. Pimp. Pig.

Scene 3

The following Sunday in the Vienna Woods

A clearing on the bank of the beautiful blue Danube. The ZAUBERKÖNIG, MARIANNE, OSKAR, VALERIE, ALFRED, various distant relatives, including ERICH from Kassel in Prussia, and a number of ugly little children dressed in white are having a picnic. All of them are grouped artistically, waiting to be photographed by OSKAR, who at the moment is fiddling with his tripod. Then he gets into position next to MARIANNE and triggers the automatic release. It all works perfectly and the group dissolves in movement.

ZAUBERKÖNIG: Wait! Again! *Da capo*! I think I moved.
OSKAR: But Papa!
ZAUBERKÖNIG: Better safe than sorry.
FIRST AUNT: That's right.
SECOND AUNT: Otherwise you'll always regret it.
ZAUBERKÖNIG: Come on, *da capo, da capo*!
OSKAR: Oh, alright, then.
  (*He busies himself with his equipment, and once again the automatic release works perfectly.*)
ZAUBERKÖNIG: That's better.
  (*The group gradually disperses.*)
FIRST AUNT: Herr Oskar, will you do me an enormous favour? Will you just take a picture of the little ones on their own, they look so sweet today.
OSKAR: Yes, of course, with pleasure.
  (*He arranges the children in a group, kissing the smallest one.*)
SECOND AUNT: (*To MARIANNE.*) Just look how good he is with children. If he wouldn't make a wonderful father, I don't know who would. He worships children, he just worships them. Oh, well, touch wood, eh?

(*She embraces MARIANNE and kisses her.*)

VALERIE: (*To ALFRED.*) Well, this is the last straw.

ALFRED: Whatever do you mean?

VALERIE: Tagging on to these people when you knew I'd be here. After everything that's passed between us.

ALFRED: What do you mean, what's passed between us? We've just split up, that's all. Doesn't mean we're not still good friends.

VALERIE: It's obvious you're not a woman. Otherwise you might have some respect for my feelings.

ALFRED: What feelings? I thought they'd changed.

VALERIE: It's not so easy for a woman to forget. There's always something inside that stays the same. Even if you are just a big swindler.

ALFRED: Look, be reasonable, will you?

VALERIE: (*Suddenly full of animosity.*) Yes, that'd just suit you, wouldn't it?

(*Silence.*)

ALFRED: May the swindler be excused now, please?

VALERIE: Who invited you today?

ALFRED: I'm not saying.

VALERIE: Not too difficult to guess, though, is it?

(*ALFRED lights a cigarette.*)

Where did we get to know each other, then? In the toyshop?

ALFRED: Shut up.

(*The ZAUBERKÖNIG approaches ALFRED with ERICH.*)

ZAUBERKÖNIG: I understand you gentlemen haven't met. May I introduce my nephew Erich, my wife's brother-in-law's son by his second marriage. And this is Herr Zentner. That's right, isn't it?

ALFRED: Yes.

ZAUBERKÖNIG: Herr von Zentner.

(*ERICH has a haversack and a canteen on his belt.*)

ERICH: Very pleased to meet you.

ZAUBERKÖNIG: Erich is a student. From Dessau.

ERICH: Kassel, Uncle.

ZAUBERKÖNIG: Kassel, Dessau, always mix them up.

(*He moves away.*)

ALFRED: (*To VALERIE.*) Do you know each other?

VALERIE: We've known each other for ages.

ERICH: We met just recently. We had a discussion about the Burgtheater and all this nonsense about the triumph of the sound film.

ALFRED: How interesting.

(*He bows formally and moves away. One of the AUNTS puts a record of 'Your Tiny Hand is Frozen' on her portable gramophone.*)

ERICH: (*Listening.*) *La Bohème.* Divine Puccini.

(*MARIANNE, now next to ALFRED, also listens.*)

MARIANNE: Your tiny hand is frozen…

ALFRED: It's *La Bohème.*

MARIANNE: Puccini.

VALERIE: (*To ERICH.*) What's your favourite operetta?

ERICH: Operettas have nothing to do with art.

VALERIE: Go on, how can you say a thing like that?

ERICH: Have you read *The Brothers Karamazov*?

VALERIE: No.

ERICH: That's art.

MARIANNE: (*To ALFRED.*) I always wanted to study eurhythmics, my ambition was to run my own institute, but my family aren't interested in anything like that. Papa always says, when a woman's financially independent from a man, it's the last step on the road to Bolshevism.

ALFRED: I don't know much about politics, but I'll tell you this: when a man's financially dependent on a woman, that's not so wonderful, either. Laws of nature, I suppose.

MARIANNE: I don't believe that.

(*OSKAR is taking photographs of the ZAUBERKÖNIG on his own, in various poses. The music has stopped.*)

ALFRED: Keen on photography, is he, your fiancé?

MARIANNE: He's obsessed with it. We've known each other for eight years.

ALFRED: How old were you when you met? I'm sorry, that just slipped out automatically.

MARIANNE: I was fourteen.

ALFRED: Not very old.

MARIANNE: I suppose we were childhood friends. He was the boy next door.

ALFRED: What if he hadn't been the boy next door?

MARIANNE: What do you mean?

ALFRED: I mean, I suppose it's all the laws of nature.
And fate.

(*Silence.*)

MARIANNE: Fate, yes. I mean, I don't think it's really what
people call love, at least, it may be as far as he's concerned,
but…as far as… (*She suddenly catches ALFRED's eye.*) No,
what am I saying, I hardly know you… God, you certainly
know how to drag it all out of a person…

ALFRED: I'm not trying to drag anything out of you. That's
the last thing I want to do.

MARIANNE: You must be a hypnotist.

OSKAR: (*To ALFRED.*) Excuse me. (*To MARIANNE.*) May I?
(*He gives her his arm and leads her towards a beautiful
group of old trees, beneath which everyone else has already
settled down for a picnic. ALFRED follows OSKAR and
MARIANNE and, like them, sits down.*)

ZAUBERKÖNIG: Now what was it we were talking about?

FIRST AUNT: The transmigration of souls.

SECOND AUNT: Transmigration of souls, what's that when
it's at home?

ERICH: It's a Buddhist idea. Part of their religious philoso-
phy. The Buddhists maintain that the soul of a dead man
passes into an animal: an elephant, say.

ZAUBERKÖNIG: Ridiculous.

ERICH: Or a snake.

FIRST AUNT: Disgusting!

ERICH: What's disgusting about it? That's just another of our
petty human prejudices. We ought to acknowledge the
secret beauty of the spider, the beetle and the centipede…

SECOND AUNT: (*Interrupting him.*) Not just before tea, if you
don't mind.

FIRST AUNT: I feel quite peculiar.

ZAUBERKÖNIG: Nothing's going to spoil my appetite today.
I don't believe in all those creepy-crawlies.

VALERIE: Stop it!
(*The ZAUBERKÖNIG rises and taps his glass with his
knife.*)

ZAUBERKÖNIG: Dear friends! Latterly it's become an open
    secret that my dear daughter Marianne has looked favour-
    ably on dear Oskar...

VALERIE: Bravo!

ZAUBERKÖNIG: Just a minute, I shan't be much longer,
    and now we've all gathered here, that's to say, I've invited
    you all here, to celebrate simply but with dignity, in a small
    but select circle, a very important moment in the lives
    of these two, now in the flower of their youth. My only
    deep regret today is that Almighty God has not spared
    Marianne's dear precious mother, God rest her soul, my
    unforgettable wife, to share this day of joy with her only
    daughter. But I'm sure of one thing, she's somewhere up
    there now in Heaven, standing behind a star and looking
    down on us. And raising her glass...
    (*He raises his glass.*) ...in a heartfelt toast to the happy and
    hereby officially engaged couple. Three cheers for the
    young couple, Oskar and Marianne, hip hip...

ALL: Hooray!

ZAUBERKÖNIG: Hip, hip...

ALL: Hooray!

ZAUBERKÖNIG: Hip, hip...

ALL: Hooray!
    (*IDA, the bright, thin, short-sighted little girl who
    complained about HAVLITSCHEK's blood-sausage, steps
    forward in front of the engaged couple, dressed in white,
    holding a bouquet, and recites. She has a speech defect.*)

IDA: Love is a very precious stone,
    It burns for ever, all alone
    And never fades away.
    It burns as long as Heaven's light
    Transfigured in Man's eyes so bright,
    Dawns with each passing day.
    (*Cheers and cries of 'How sweet!' etc., as IDA hands
    MARIANNE the bouquet with a curtsey. Then everyone
    caresses IDA and congratulates the happy couple in the
    highest of spirits. The portable gramophone strikes up with
    the 'Wedding March', and the ZAUBERKÖNIG kisses*

MARIANNE on the forehead and OSKAR on the mouth.
Then he wipes the tears from his eyes and lies down in his
hammock. Meanwhile, ERICH and OSKAR have drunk
a toast of friendship from ERICH's canteen.)

ERICH: Ladies and gentlemen, your attention, please! Oskar
and Marianne! I'm going to take the liberty of drinking a
very special toast to you from my canteen here. Good luck,
good health and a lot of good upstanding German children!
Cheers!

VALERIE: (*Tipsy.*) And no niggers, eh? Cheers! *Sieg Heil!*

ERICH: Excuse me, Madame, but I'm afraid this is one subject on which I cannot allow frivolous remarks. As far as
I'm concerned the subject is sacred. You know my position
vis-à-vis our racial problems.

VALERIE: Problems, problems. Wait, don't go away, you
difficult man, you…

ERICH: Difficult. What do you mean?

VALERIE: Interesting…

ERICH: In what way?

VALERIE: You think I like the Jews? You big baby…
(*She links arms with the big baby and drags him off.*
Everyone settles down in the wood, and the little children
play and do their best to disturb them. OSKAR plays the
lute and sings.)

OSKAR: *Sei gepriesen, du lauschige Nacht,*
Hast zwei Herzen so glücklich gemacht.
Und die Rosen im folgenden Jahr
Sahn ein Paar am Altar!
Auch der Klapperstorch blieb nicht lang aus,
Brachte klappernd den Segen ins Haus.
Und entschwand auch der liebliche Mai,
In der Jugend erblüht er neu!
(*He plays the song through again, humming instead of*
singing. Everyone else, except for ALFRED and MARI-
ANNE, joins in, humming along with him. ALFRED
approaches MARIANNE.)

ALFRED: May I congratulate you again?

(*MARIANNE closes her eyes. ALFRED gives her hand a lingering kiss. OSKAR has been watching, has handed his lute to the SECOND AUNT, crept over to them and now stands next to MARIANNE.*)

(*Formally.*) Congratulations.

OSKAR: Thank you.

(*ALFRED bows formally and moves away. OSKAR watches him go.*)

He's jealous of me. He's got no manners. Who is he, anyway? ·

MARIANNE: A customer.

OSKAR: Since when?

MARIANNE: He came in yesterday, and we talked for a bit, not for long, and I invited him. He bought a game.

VALERIE: (*Shrilly.*) I have a forfeit, what's my forfeit?

ERICH: It's you have to moo three times.

VALERIE: Auntie Henriette, you're it, Auntie Henriette.

(*The FIRST AUNT strikes a pose and bellows.*)

FIRST AUNT: Moo! Moo! Moo!

(*Loud laughter.*)

VALERIE: And I have a forfeit, what's my forfeit?

ZAUBERKÖNIG: You have to baa three times.

VALERIE: Well, you're it.

ZAUBERKÖNIG: Baa! Baa! Baa!

(*Howls of laughter.*)

VALERIE: And I have a forfeit, what's my forfeit?

SECOND AUNT: It's you have to give a demonstration.

ERICH: What of?

SECOND AUNT: Whatever you can.

VALERIE: Oskar! Hear that, Oskar? You have to give us a demonstration.

ERICH: Anything you like.

ZAUBERKÖNIG: Whatever you can do.

(*Silence.*)

OSKAR: Ladies and gentlemen, I'm going to give you a demonstration of something really useful. I've been studying the Japanese method of self-defence. What they call ju-jitsu. Now, pay attention, please, this is the easiest way to disarm your opponent.

(*He suddenly lunges at MARIANNE and demonstrates his hold on her, throwing her to the ground.*)

MARIANNE: Ow! Ow! Ow!

FIRST AUNT: Don't be so rough.

ZAUBERKÖNIG: Bravo! Bravissimo!

OSKAR: (*To the FIRST AUNT.*) It was only a pretend throw, otherwise I could have damaged her spine.

FIRST AUNT: Well, that's nice, isn't it?

ZAUBERKÖNIG: (*Slapping OSKAR on the back.*) Very clever! Very well illustrated!

SECOND AUNT: (*Helping MARIANNE up.*) You're such a delicate plant. Well, now, have you another forfeit?

VALERIE: Afraid not. All gone. That's the lot.

ZAUBERKÖNIG: Then I have a suggestion. Let's all go for a swim. In the river, it'll be nice and cool. I'm sweating like a boiled monkey.

ERICH: Excellent idea.

VALERIE: But where are the ladies going to change?

ZAUBERKÖNIG: Nothing could be simpler. Ladies to the right, gentlemen to the left. And we'll meet again in the beautiful blue Danube.

(*The portable gramophone is playing 'The Blue Danube Waltz' and the ladies disappear to the right, the gentlemen to the left. VALERIE and ALFRED are the last to leave.*)

VALERIE: Alfred.

ALFRED: Yes?

(*VALERIE hums along with the waltz tune and takes her blouse off.*)

What?

(*VALERIE throws him a kiss.*)

Goodbye.

VALERIE: Wait a minute. What does the young sir think of the bride to be?

(*ALFRED looks at her, then goes up to her quickly and stops just in front of her.*)

ALFRED: Breathe out.

VALERIE: Whatever for?

ALFRED: Breathe out!

(*VALERIE breathes on him.*)
Old soak!

VALERIE: Just a bit merry, that's all, what are you, a vegetarian? Man proposes and God disposes. It's not every day there's an engagement party...or is it a disengagement party, you swine?

ALFRED: There's no need to take that tone.

VALERIE: Don't you touch me, don't you dare lay a finger on me.

ALFRED: When have I ever laid a finger on you?

VALERIE: The seventeenth of March.

(*Silence.*)

ALFRED: Well, you have got a memory, haven't you?

VALERIE: I remember everything. Good and bad.
(*She suddenly holds the blouse up in front of her.*) Now go away, I want to get undressed!

ALFRED: Well, that wouldn't be much of a surprise for me, would it?

VALERIE: (*Shrieking.*) Stop staring at me. Go away! Go away!

ALFRED: Hysterical cow.
(*He exits, left. VALERIE, alone, watches him go.*)

VALERIE: Bastard. Shit. Rat. Pig.
(*She undresses. The ZAUBERKÖNIG emerges from behind the bushes in his swimsuit and watches her. VALERIE, now only in slip, underwear and stockings, notices him.*)
Jesus, Mary and Joseph! Oo, you wicked creature! Peeping Tom, that's what you are.

ZAUBERKÖNIG: Now, now, I'm not a pervert. Don't worry about me, just carry on undressing.

VALERIE: I do have my modesty, you know.

ZAUBERKÖNIG: Go on, nobody worries about that sort of thing these days.

VALERIE: Yes, I know, but I have such a vivid imagination...
(*She skips behind a bush. The ZAUBERKÖNIG sits down in front of the bush, finds VALERIE's corset, picks it up and sniffs it.*)

ZAUBERKÖNIG: Imagination or no imagination, these days, it seems to me, the world's going mad. No loyalty, no beliefs, no moral principles. Everything's collapsing, nothing's certain any more. Ready for the Flood. (*He lays the corset aside, the smell is obviously nothing to write home about.*) I'm just happy to have settled Marianne, you can always rely on a butcher's shop.

VALERIE: What about a tobacconist's?

ZAUBERKÖNIG: Oh, yes. Smoking, eating, there'll always be a demand for that...but magic? When I think about the future, I get very pessimistic sometimes. I haven't had it easy in my life, not at all easy, you've only got to think of my dear wife, all that endless bother with the specialists...

(*VALERIE appears in a woollen bathing costume, fiddling with her straps.*)

VALERIE: What did she actually die of?

ZAUBERKÖNIG: (*Staring at her bosom.*) Breasts.

VALERIE: Not cancer?

ZAUBERKÖNIG: That's right. Cancer.

VALERIE: Poor thing.

ZAUBERKÖNIG: Well, it wasn't very nice for me, either. The left one, she had to have off. She never was very healthy, but of course her parents never told me. When I look at you, though, by comparison: imposing, I'd go as far as to say regal. A regal figure.

(*VALERIE touches her toes a few times.*)

VALERIE: You men, what do you know about the tragedy of women? If we didn't spend all our time doing ourselves up and taking care of our appearances...

ZAUBERKÖNIG: (*Interrupting her.*) Don't you think I have to take care of my appearance?

VALERIE: Of course. But with a man it's the inner qualities you look for first.

(*She does a bit of eurhythmics. The ZAUBERKÖNIG watches her and starts doing knee-bends.*)

That's enough, I'm worn out.

(*She throws herself down next to him.*)

ZAUBERKÖNIG: The dying swan.

(*He sits down next to her. Silence.*)

VALERIE: May I rest my head in your lap?

ZAUBERKÖNIG: In the garden there is no sin.

VALERIE: (*Doing so.*) It's still very hard, the earth...it's been such a long winter.
(*Silence.*)
(*Softly.*) You. How do you feel? When the sun shines on my skin like this, I always get so, I don't know...
ZAUBERKÖNIG: So...what?
(*Silence.*)
VALERIE: I saw you playing with my corset just now.
(*Silence.*)
ZAUBERKÖNIG: What about it?
VALERIE: What about it?
(*The ZAUBERKÖNIG suddenly throws himself on her and kisses her.*)
My God, you're so impetuous. I never would have thought it of you...you naughty man, you...
ZAUBERKÖNIG: Am I naughty? Am I naughty?
VALERIE: Yes...no, you're...stop it, someone's coming!
(*They roll apart. ERICH enters in a swimming costume with an air-gun.*)
ERICH: Excuse me, Uncle. Do you mind if I do some shooting?
ZAUBERKÖNIG: What do you want to do?
ERICH: Shoot.
ZAUBERKÖNIG: You want to shoot? Here?
ERICH: Yes, at the target on that beech over there.
The monthly competition of our student cadet corps is the day after tomorrow, and I just thought I'd get in some practice, if you don't mind. May I?
VALERIE: Of course.
ZAUBERKÖNIG: Of course? (*To VALERIE.*) Of course!
(*He gets up.*) The cadet corps. Oh, yes, of course! You mustn't forget how to shoot, whatever you do. Personally, I'm going to get cooled down. In the beautiful blue Danube. (*Aside.*) Hang yourselves, all I care. (*He exits. ERICH loads, aims and fires. VALERIE watches him, speaks after the third shot.*)
VALERIE: Excuse me, I don't mean to interfere with you, but what is it you're studying at the moment?
ERICH: Law. Third term. (*He aims.*) Industrial law. (*He fires.*)

VALERIE: Industrial law. Isn't that rather boring?

ERICH: (*Loading.*) Good prospects. One day I should be a
corporation lawyer. (*He aims.*) In industry. (*He fires.*)

VALERIE: And what do you think of our Vienna?

ERICH: Magnificently baroque.

VALERIE: And what about the sweet little Viennese girls?

ERICH: To be quite frank, I don't get on very well with young
girls. Actually, I've already been engaged, but
I was bitterly disillusioned, because Käthe was just too
young to be able to bring the right kind of understanding to
bear on the problems of my ego. With young girls you're
wasting your feelings at the wrong address. I'd much rather
someone more mature, someone who can give as well as
take. (*He fires.*)

VALERIE: Where are you living?

ERICH: I'm thinking of moving.

VALERIE: I might have a furnished room.

ERICH: Cheap?

VALERIE: Dirt cheap.

ERICH: That'd be splendid. (*He fires.*)

VALERIE: Well, Mr Corporation Lawyer...go on, let me have
a go.

ERICH: My pleasure.

VALERIE: No, my pleasure. (*She takes the gun from him.*)
Did you fight in the war?

ERICH: Alas, no. I was born in nineteen eleven.

VALERIE: Nineteen eleven. (*She takes a long time aiming.*)

ERICH: (*Giving the commands.*) Attention! Take aim! Fire!
(*VALERIE doesn't fire. She lowers the gun slowly and
looks at him intently.*)
What's the matter?

VALERIE: Ow! (*Suddenly, she doubles up, whimpering.*) I get
these shooting pains. My poor kidneys...
(*Silence.*)

ERICH: Is there anything I can do?

VALERIE: No, thanks. I'm all right now. It quite often
happens when I get excited. I always suffer for it. I don't
know what I'm aiming at any more...

ERICH: (*Confused.*) What do you mean, what you're aiming at?

VALERIE: That's because it's getting dark.

(*She embraces him, he lets it happen. They kiss.*)

It's always worth trying to get what you're aiming at.

If you've nothing to aim for, you're not human any more.

You. Mr Nineteen hundred and eleven.

Scene 4

By the beautiful blue Danube

By now, the sun has gone down, it's already getting dark, and in the distance auntie's portable gramophone is playing Johann Strauss's waltz 'Frühlingsstimmen'.

ALFRED, in a bathrobe and straw hat, is staring dreamily across at the opposite bank. MARIANNE climbs out of the beautiful blue Danube and sees ALFRED. Silence. ALFRED lifts his hat.

ALFRED: I knew you'd come ashore here.

MARIANNE: How did you know?

ALFRED: I just knew.

(*Silence.*)

MARIANNE: The Danube's so soft, it's like velvet.

ALFRED: Like velvet.

MARIANNE: I'd like to be somewhere else, far away, today.

Tonight you could sleep out in the open.

ALFRED: Easily.

MARIANNE: Oh, we're just slaves of civilisation.

What's become of our real natures?

ALFRED: We've turned our real natures into a strait-jacket.

Nobody's allowed to do what they want to do.

MARIANNE: And nobody wants to do what they're allowed to do.

(*Silence.*)

ALFRED: And nobody's allowed to do what they're able to do.

MARIANNE: And nobody's able to do what they ought to do.

(*ALFRED embraces her dramatically and she makes no move to resist him. A long kiss.*)

(*Gets her breath.*) I knew it, I knew it...

ALFRED: So did I.

MARIANNE: Do you love me the way you ought to...?

ALFRED: I feel as if I do. Let's sit down.

(*They sit down. Silence.*)

MARIANNE: I'm so glad you're not stupid. I mean, I'm surrounded by nothing but stupid people. Even Papa's not what you'd call a bright spark. And sometimes I think he just wants to use me to revenge himself on my poor dear mother. She was very stubborn, you see.

ALFRED: You think too much.

MARIANNE: I'm feeling good now. I feel like singing. I always want to sing when I'm sad. (*She starts humming and then stops again.*) Why aren't you saying anything?

(*Silence.*)

ALFRED: Do you love me?

MARIANNE: Very much.

ALFRED: The way you ought to? I mean, sensibly?

MARIANNE: Sensibly?

ALFRED: I mean, I wouldn't like you to do anything rash. I couldn't take the responsibility.

MARIANNE: Don't brood, there's no need to brood, look at the stars. They'll still be up there in the sky when we're lying down here in the earth.

ALFRED: I'm going to be cremated.

MARIANNE: So am I. You're...oh, you're...you...

(*Silence.*)

You've...you've struck me like lightning and split me in two. But now I know. I know for certain.

ALFRED: What?

MARIANNE: That I'm not going to marry him.

ALFRED: Marianne!

MARIANNE: What's the matter?

(*Silence.*)

ALFRED: I haven't any money.

MARIANNE: What's that got to do with it?

ALFRED: It's my absolute basic duty. I've never destroyed someone's engagement, never in my life. On principle.

Falling in love, yes, but making people split up because of it, no, I just don't have the moral right. I feel that way on principle.

(*Silence.*)

MARIANNE: I was right about you, you are a sensitive man. Now I feel doubly yours. I just don't suit Oskar and that's all there is to it.

(*Meanwhile, it's got dark and fireworks are being set off nearby.*)

ALFRED: Rockets. To celebrate your engagement.

MARIANNE: To celebrate our engagement.

ALFRED: And Bengal lights.

MARIANNE: Blue, green, yellow, red…

ALFRED: They'll be out looking for you.

MARIANNE: I don't care if they find us. Stay with me, you've been sent down from Heaven, you're my guardian angel…

(*Bengal lights – blue, green, yellow, red – go up and light up ALFRED and MARIANNE and the ZAUBERKÖNIG, who is standing in front of them with his hand on his heart. MARIANNE stifles a cry. Silence. ALFRED goes up to the ZAUBERKÖNIG.*)

ALFRED: Herr Zauberkönig…

ZAUBERKÖNIG: (*Interrupting him.*) Be quiet! You don't need to explain, I've heard everything. This is an absolute scandal! On the day of the engagement! Lying around naked! That's very nice, isn't it? Marianne! Get dressed! Suppose Oskar comes. Jesus, Mary and Joseph preserve us!

ALFRED: Naturally I shall take the consequences, if necessary.

ZAUBERKÖNIG: There'll be no consequences. All you have to do, you…sir, is run for it. I will not allow this engagement to be ruined, for moral reasons or any other reasons. So you'd better make sure no-one finds out about this, you good-for-nothing. Promise me on your word of honour.

ALFRED: I promise.

MARIANNE: No!

ZAUBERKÖNIG: (*Through his teeth.*) Will you not shout! Are you ready? Hurry up and get dressed, come on, at the double. You slut!

(*OSKAR appears and takes in the situation at a glance.*)

OSKAR: Marianne! Marianne!

ZAUBERKÖNIG: Disaster!

(*Silence.*)

ALFRED: Your fiancé's been swimming, she's only just this minute come out.

MARIANNE: Don't lie! Just don't tell lies! I haven't been swimming, I've no intention of going swimming. I'm not going to let myself be tyrannised by you. The slave is snapping her chains...there! (*She throws her engagement ring in OSKAR's face.*) I'm not going to let my life be ruined, it's my life! At the last minute God has sent me this man. So I'm not, I'm not going to marry you, I'm not going to marry you, I'm not going to marry you! As far as I'm concerned, the toyshop can sink into the ground, and the sooner the better!

ZAUBERKÖNIG: My only child! I'll remember that! (*Silence. During MARIANNE's outburst, the other picnickers have appeared and are listening with malicious interest. OSKAR steps up to MARIANNE.*)

OSKAR: Marianne, I hope you'll never have to go through what's happening to me now. I'm going to go on loving you, you won't escape from me. And thank you for everything. (*He exits. Silence.*)

ZAUBERKÖNIG: (*To ALFRED.*) Who do you think you are?

ALFRED: Me?

VALERIE: Nothing. He's a nothing.

ZAUBERKÖNIG: A nothing. On top of everything else. Well, I don't have a daughter any more. (*He exits with the picnickers. ALFRED and MARIANNE are alone. The moon is shining.*)

ALFRED: I'm sorry. Forgive me... (*MARIANNE gives him her hand.*) ...for not having wanted you just now, I mean. I feel responsible, that's what was responsible for it. I'm not worthy of your love, I can't offer you any sort of a life, I'm not really a man at all...

MARIANNE: Nothing's going to shake me now. Let me make you into a man. You make me feel so big and important...

ALFRED: And you give me a kind of uplift. On the spiritual plane I feel really small compared to you.

MARIANNE: You bring me out of myself, I'm watching myself go. See, I'm really far away from myself now. I'm right back there, I can hardly see myself any more. I want to have your child…

End of Act One.

ACT TWO

Scene 1

Back in the quiet street in Vienna 8, in front of OSKAR's butcher's shop, the dolls' hospital and VALERIE's tobacconist's. The sun is shining as before, and upstairs the schoolgirl is still playing Johann Strauss's 'Tales from the Vienna Woods'.

HAVLITSCHEK is standing in the doorway of the butcher's, devouring a sausage. EMMA, a girl who's ready for anything, is standing next to him, holding a shopping-bag and listening to the music.

EMMA: Herr Havlitschek...
HAVLITSCHEK: What can I do you for?
EMMA: There's something nice about music, isn't there?
HAVLITSCHEK: I can think of something a good deal nicer, Fräulein Emma.
    (*EMMA hums along quietly with the waltz.*)
    But that needs some work from your end, eh, Fräulein Emma?
EMMA: I think you're a bit of a Casanova, Herr Havlitschek.
HAVLITSCHEK: You can call me Ladislaus it you like.
    (*Pause.*)
EMMA: I had a dream about your Herr Oskar last night.
HAVLITSCHEK: Can't you find nothing more exciting to dream about than that?
EMMA: He's got them great big sad eyes, Herr Oskar.
    It really upsets you when he looks at you.
HAVLITSCHEK: That's what love does for you.
EMMA: How do you mean?
HAVLITSCHEK: What I mean is, he fell in love with this bit of shoddy goods, and she just up and left him, must be a year ago now, and went off with some other bit of shoddy goods.
EMMA: And he still loves her? I think that's nice.
HAVLITSCHEK: I think it's bloody ridiculous.

EMMA: A grand passion, there's something romantic
about it…

HAVLITSCHEK: There's something sick about it, ask me.
Just look at the way he looks, he's torturing himself.
He won't look twice at another woman, and all the while
he's worth a packet and he's a well set-up bloke, he could
marry any one of a dozen women, and not one of them
rubbish, any time he felt like it. But no, he's stuck on that
little bitch on heat. Christ knows what he does for it.

EMMA: How do you mean, Herr Havlitschek?

HAVLITSCHEK: Well, I mean, I can't think how he sweats
it off.

EMMA: Oo, you are disgusting.
(*Pause.*)

HAVLITSCHEK: I'm off tomorrow, Fräulein Emma,
and I shall be at the sixty-eight bus terminus.

EMMA: I can't manage before three.

HAVLITSCHEK: No problem.
(*Pause.*)

EMMA: Half past three, then. And don't forget what you
promised, you said you wouldn't be naughty, Ladislaus…
(*She exits. HAVLITSCHEK watches her go and spits out
the sausage-skin.*)

HAVLITSCHEK: Stupid bitch, stupid…
(*OSKAR steps out of the butcher's.*)

OSKAR: Don't forget, will you? We have to stick the pig
today. You do it, I don't really fancy it today.
(*Pause.*)

HAVLITSCHEK: May I have a word with you, Herr Oskar,
you don't mind if I say what I think, do you?

OSKAR: Is it about the pig?

HAVLITSCHEK: More of a sow than a pig, really. Herr
Oskar, don't take it to heart like this, please, all this with
your old fiancée, look, women, they're common as dirt.
Anyone can get a woman, cripples, anyone, even if they're
falling apart with the pox. And where it counts they're
all the same, women, believe me, I'm being honest with
you. They got no soul, women, it's just surface meat. And
you shouldn't spoil a woman either, that's a big mistake,

all they need's a good punch in the mouth every now and then, something like that.

(*Pause.*)

OSKAR: Woman is an enigma, Havlitschek. Like the Sphinx. I've taken samples of Marianne's handwriting round to various graphologists. The first one said, ah, this is the handwriting of a vampire, the second one said she'd make a really good friend, and the third one said she's the ideal housewife personified. An angel.

Scene 2

A furnished room in Vienna 18

Extremely cheap. About seven o'clock in the morning. ALFRED is still in bed, smoking a cigarette. MARIANNE is cleaning her teeth. An old pram in the corner and nappies hanging on the line. Grey day, dim light.

MARIANNE: (*Gargling.*) You once said I was an angel. I told you then I wasn't an angel, I was just an ordinary girl with no ambitions. But you're so cold and calculating.

ALFRED: I'm not calculating, you know I'm not.

MARIANNE: Yes, you are. (*She fixes her hair.*) I must get a haircut.

ALFRED: So must I.

(*Silence.*)

Marianne. What you getting up so early for?

MARIANNE: Because I can't sleep.

(*Silence.*)

ALFRED: Are you unhappy?

MARIANNE: Aren't you?

(*They stare at each other.*)

ALFRED: Who was it ruined the racing for me? I haven't spoken to a bookmaker, let alone a tipster, for a whole year. So I'm buggered there, aren't I? A new season, new favourites, two-year-olds, three-year-olds…there's a new generation I have no contact with at all. And why don't I? Because I have to flog my guts out trying to sell a skin cream nobody buys, because it's muck.

MARIANNE: People just don't have any money.

ALFRED: That's right, make excuses for people.

MARIANNE: You can't help it, I'm not blaming you.

ALFRED: I should bloody well hope not!

MARIANNE: Well, it's hardly my fault, the economic crisis.

ALFRED: Oh, you're so selfish. Who was it came up with the insane idea I should spend my life rushing round trying to sell cosmetics? It was you. (*He gets out of bed.*) Where are my suspenders?

(*MARIANNE points to a chair.*)

MARIANNE: There.

ALFRED: No.

MARIANNE: Then they're on the bedside cabinet.

ALFRED: No.

MARIANNE: Then I don't know where they are.

ALFRED: It's your job to know where they are.

MARIANNE: You're just like Papa.

ALFRED: Will you stop comparing me with that old moron!

MARIANNE: Don't shout! If you wake the baby, it'll finish me, all that crying.

(*Silence.*)

ALFRED: And that's another thing, something's got to be done about the baby. We can't just sit here, all three of us, rotting in this hole. The baby's going to have to go.

MARIANNE: The baby's staying right here.

ALFRED: The baby's got to go.

MARIANNE: No. Never.

(*Silence.*)

ALFRED: Where are my suspenders?

(*MARIANNE looks at him, wide-eyed.*)

MARIANNE: Do you know what day it is today?

ALFRED: No.

MARIANNE: It's the twelfth.

(*Silence.*)

ALFRED: So what?

MARIANNE: It's our anniversary. A year ago today I saw you for the first time. In the window.

ALFRED: I don't know why you always have to talk in hiero-
glyphics. We're not Egyptians, you know. What window?
MARIANNE: I was just arranging the skeleton and you
knocked on the window. And then I let the blind down,
because I suddenly got scared.
ALFRED: That's right.
MARIANNE: I was very lonely... (*She starts weeping, softly.*)
ALFRED: Look, don't start snivelling again... Listen,
Marianne, I understand your maternal possessiveness a
hundred per cent, but it's in the baby's interest to get him
out of this damp hole. It's so grey and gloomy here, and at
my mother's out in the Wachau, it's sunny.
MARIANNE: Well...
ALFRED: That's settled, then.
(*Silence.*)
MARIANNE: Fate weaves the pattern of our lives...
(*She suddenly stares at ALFRED.*) What did you say?
ALFRED: What?
MARIANNE: You said, stupid cow.
ALFRED: What are you talking about?
MARIANNE: Don't deny it!
(*ALFRED is cleaning his teeth and gargling.*)
You ought not to insult me all the time.
(*Silence. ALFRED is putting shaving cream on his face.*)
ALFRED: My dear child, if there's one thing I hate from the
bottom of my heart, it's stupidity. And sometimes you are
quite outstandingly stupid. I can't understand why you're
so stupid. It's not necessary, you know, to be so stupid.
(*Silence.*)
MARIANNE: You once said I gave you a kind of uplift...
on the spiritual plane...
ALFRED: I never said that. I can't possibly have said that.
And if I did, I was wrong.
MARIANNE: Alfred!
ALFRED: Don't shout! Remember the baby.
MARIANNE: I'm so frightened, Alfred...
ALFRED: You're imagining things.
MARIANNE: I mean, if you've really forgotten everything
already...
ALFRED: Crap!

Scene 3

A small café in Vienna 2

HIERLINGER is playing billiards against himself. ALFRED enters.

HIERLINGER: Hello, Alfred! Good to see you again. Bit of a long face, why's that?

ALFRED: I've got a lot of worries.

HIERLINGER: Worrying never did anyone any good. Come on, give us a game, take your mind off it. (*He hands him a cue.*) First one to fifty, you break.

ALFRED: *Bon.* (*He miscues.*) Pathetic.

HIERLINGER: (*Taking his shot.*) Is it true you're working in the bank again?

ALFRED: Nothing else going.

HIERLINGER: *Cherchez la femme!* When you fall in love, your brains are in your arse.

ALFRED: My dear Ferdinand, it's not a question of brains or keeping a cool head, it's to do with quite another organ. (*He puts his hand on his heart.*) There's a story by Hans Christian Andersen about the wicked boy shooting an arrow right into some poor old poet's heart. Cupid, Ferdinand, the god Cupid.

HIERLINGER: (*Concentrating on his break.*) Should have pulled it out again.

ALFRED: Thing is, I'm very soft-hearted, and she appealed to my youthful idealism. To start with, there was a certain amount of standard passion involved, and then, when the initial attraction had worn off, I started to feel sorry for her. I mean, she's the type of girl the right man wouldn't mind mothering, although she can be a spiteful little bitch sometimes. My God, I think I'm infatuated with her.

HIERLINGER: Infatuation's something in your blood. It's something to do with blood-heat.

ALFRED: Is that true?

HIERLINGER: Course it is. You're on. Eleven.
(*ALFRED plays a shot.*)

Alfred. Do you know what really knocked me back?
Having a baby in the middle of the depression...

ALFRED: Well, God knows, I never wanted her to have
a baby, the whole thing was her idea and it just sort of
happened. I would have got rid of it straight away, no
trouble at all, but she wouldn't have that, she was quite
fanatical about it, and then I had to lean on her very
heavily before I could persuade her to go through with it...
and what a pantomime that turned out to be! Worse than
useless and it still cost us a fortune. My God. You can't
expect anything but bad luck and you just have to put up
with it.

(*MARIANNE appears. ALFRED sees her and calls over
to her.*)

Sit over there, will you? I'm just finishing my game.

(*MARIANNE sits at a table and leafs through fashion
magazines. Silence.*)

HIERLINGER: Is that your lady?

ALFRED: Yup.

(*Silence.*)

HIERLINGER: So that's your lady. Funny. My good friend
Alfred's been living with a girl like that for over a year
now and this is the first time I've clapped eyes on her.
I thought it was only supposed to be the jealous Turks
who kept their favourites locked away from their best
friends.

ALFRED: In this case it's the other way round. It's not me, it's
her who's cut me off from my best friends...

HIERLINGER: (*Interrupting him.*) By the way, what's her
name?

ALFRED: Marianne.

(*Silence.*)

What do you think?

HIERLINGER: I pictured her different.

ALFRED: In what way?

HIERLINGER: Bit more buxom.

ALFRED: More buxom than that?

HIERLINGER: Don't know why. You can't help it, you get
these pictures in your mind.

(*Silence.*)

ALFRED: She is quite buxom. Buxomer than you'd think.

(*Silence.*)

HIERLINGER: Bloody hell, that was a monumentally
stupid thing to do, wasn't it, breaking up with the mad
tobacconist. You'd've been well stocked and fancy free.

ALFRED: No sense going on about the past. You'd be
better off helping me get out of this disastrous set-up as
painlessly as possible for all concerned.

HIERLINGER: Easier said than done. I don't suppose it's a
bed of roses, I mean financially speaking.

ALFRED: It's a bed of thorns, Ferdinand. A bed of thorns and
stinging nettles, like old Job had.

HIERLINGER: Where's the baby?

ALFRED: At my mother's. Out in the Wachau. At last!

HIERLINGER: Well, that's a help. Now the next thing
I would try and do is fix your Marianne up with something
that'll make her financially independent, find some way of
sticking her into some profession. It's well known that when
a woman has a profession, it gradually undermines any
kind of relationship, even marriage. That's the Church's
main argument, that's why they're fighting against women
getting jobs, because the effect is to break up the family.
They're not idiots, you know, the cardinals, they're the
crème de la crème, they're the cleverest people we've got.

ALFRED: Yes, I know. But Marianne's not trained for any profession. The only thing she's interested in is eurhythmics.

HIERLINGER: Big demand for eurhythmics.

ALFRED: Is that true?

HIERLINGER: Course it is.

ALFRED: I don't think I'm capable of thinking any more.

HIERLINGER: After all, eurhythmics is really only
an offshoot of dancing, and that could be the light
at the end of the tunnel. See, I have a friend in
the dancing world, a baroness with international
connections, who puts together ballets and that kind of
thing for very classy establishments, might well be a possibility there. Apart from anything else, the baroness owes
me a favour.

ALFRED: Well, I'd be eternally grateful to you…

HIERLINGER: I'm your friend, that's good enough for me. Tell you what, if I go now, I can catch the baroness at her bridge party. So, I'll see you, Alfred. Do me a favour, settle up for the coffee, will you? Chin up, you'll be hearing from me, everything'll be all right.

(*He exits. ALFRED, holding his cue, slowly approaches MARIANNE and sits at her table.*)

MARIANNE: Who won?

ALFRED: I lost. That's because I'm lucky in love. (*He smiles, then suddenly stares at her neck.*) What's that?

MARIANNE: This? It's a lucky charm.

ALFRED: What kind of a lucky charm?

MARIANNE: It's St Anthony.

ALFRED: St Anthony? How long have you had that?

(*Silence.*)

MARIANNE: Since I was little, whenever I lost anything, I just had to say, St Anthony, help me, and I'd find it again.

(*Silence.*)

ALFRED: Is that supposed to be symbolic?

MARIANNE: It was just…

(*Silence.*)

ALFRED: Personally I don't believe in a life after death, although of course I believe in a Higher Being, that's obvious, otherwise we wouldn't be here. Anyway, St. Anthony, you listen to this, I've got something to tell you, might turn out to be important…

Scene 4

At home with the Baroness
with international connections

HELENE, the BARONESS's blind sister, is sitting in the drawing-room at the spinet, improvising. HIERLINGER enters with MARIANNE, shown in by the SERVANT. HELENE breaks off her improvisation.

HELENE: Anna! Who's that?

SERVANT: It's Herr von Hierlinger and a young lady.

HIERLINGER: *Enchanté*, countess.

(*HELENE stands up and gropes her way towards him.*)

HELENE: Oh, good afternoon, Herr von Hierlinger. How very nice to see you again…

HIERLINGER: Pleasure's all mine, countess. Is the baroness in?

HELENE: Yes, my sister's at home, but at the moment she's busy with the plumber. I put something I shouldn't have down the drain the other day and everything's blocked up. Who's that you've brought with you, Herr von Hierlinger?

HIERLINGER: A young lady with a great interest in eurhythmics. The baroness knows about her already. May I introduce…

HELENE: (*Interrupting him.*) Very pleased to meet you! I'm afraid I can't see you, but you have a very sympathetic hand. Leave me your hand a minute, little lady of the hand…

HIERLINGER: Countess Helene has an amazing talent for palm-reading.

(*Silence.*)

MARIANNE: What sort of hand have I got?

(*HELENE is still holding her tightly by the hand.*)

HELENE: It's not as simple as that, my dear, when you're blind you have to use your sense of touch to find your way around. You have not much experience behind you, much more to come…

MARIANNE: What sort of thing?

(*The BARONESS enters unnoticed, wearing a cosmetic face- mask, and listens.*)

HELENE: I would almost go so far as to say, this is the hand of a sensualist. You have a child as well, don't you?

MARIANNE: Yes.

HIERLINGER: Fantastic! Fantastic!

HELENE: Boy or girl?

MARIANNE: Boy.

(*Silence.*)

HELENE: Yes, your son's going to give you a lot of joy.
He's going to turn out all right.
MARIANNE: (*Smiling.*) Really?
BARONESS: Helene! What is all this nonsense? You're not
a gypsy! You'd be better off trying not to block up the
lavatory again, my God, the filth out there! You reading
palms! That's a paradox, if ever I heard one.
(*She takes off her face-mask.*)
HELENE: Oh, I have my premonitions.
BARONESS: Well, be so good as to confine your
premonitions to the lavatory. It's costing me five schillings
again to get all that filth cleaned up! Anyone would think I
was living off you, not you off me!
(*Silence.*)
Well, Hierlinger dear, I expect this is the young lady you
telephoned me about the day before yesterday.
HIERLINGER: That's right. (*Quietly.*) And don't forget, one
good turn deserves another.
(*The BARONESS threatens him playfully, shaking her
fore-finger at him.*)
BARONESS: Blackmail?
HIERLINGER: Don't point, it's rude to point.
BARONESS: I know you're a man of honour. (*She leaves him
looking poisonously at her, crosses to MARIANNE and walks
round her, studying her from every angle.*) Hm. Well, Fräulein,
you say you have a great interest in eurhythmics?
MARIANNE: Yes.
BARONESS: And you'd like to find some practical use for
your interest?
MARIANNE: Yes.
BARONESS: Can you sing?
MARIANNE: Sing?
BARONESS: I operate on the principle that there's no such
thing as can't. You can do anything if you set your mind
to it! The dance groups I put together are international
attractions at first-class night-clubs. So you can't sing?
MARIANNE: I'm afraid...
BARONESS: Didn't you learn to sing at school?

MARIANNE: Oh, yes.

BARONESS: Well, then! I just want to hear your voice. Surely you know a nice Viennese song, you're Viennese, aren't you? Some nice folksong…

MARIANNE: What about the 'Song of the Wachau'?

BARONESS: That'll be fine. Off you go. 'The Song of the Wachau'.

(*MARIANNE sings, HELENE at the spinet.*)

MARIANNE: *Es kam einst gezogen ein Bursch ganz allein*
Und wanderte froh in den Abend hinein.
Da flog ein Lächeln ihm zu und ein Blick.
Er dachte noch lange daran zurück.
Ein rosiges Antlitz, ein goldener Schopf,
Zwei leuchtende Augen, ein Mädchenkopf.
Das Mädel, das ging ihm nicht mehr aus dem Sinn,
Und oft sang er vor sich hin:

Da draussen in der Wachau
Die Donau fliesst so blau,
Steht einsam ein Winzerhaus,
Da schaut ein Mädel heraus.
Hat Lippen rot wie Blut,
Und küssen kanns so gut,
Die Augen sind veilchenblau
Vom Mädel in der Wachau.

Scene 5

Out in the Wachau

Here too the sun is shining as before, only now an old pram stands in front of the cottage.

MOTHER: (*To ALFRED.*) He looks just like you, little Leopold. And he doesn't cry much either. You were very good too, when you were a baby.

ALFRED: I'm just glad I haven't got him in Vienna. He'll do much better out here in the good air, than he would have done living in our barracks.

MOTHER: Has Marianne started at the ballet yet?

ALFRED: No, not till next Saturday.

(*Silence.*)

MOTHER: (*Anxiously.*) You used to say if you had a child you'd get married. Do you still feel the same way?

ALFRED: You used to say I could make a good match.

(*Silence.*)

MOTHER: Well, naturally this particular relationship is rather unfortunate.

ALFRED: May I have a word with Granny now?

MOTHER: I'll go and tell her. I have to go back to the cellar now anyway.

(*She exits into the cottage. ALFRED, alone, bends over the pram and contemplates his child. His GRANDMOTHER emerges from the cottage.*)

GRANDMOTHER: What can I do for you, young man?

ALFRED: Have you thought about it?

GRANDMOTHER: I don't have any money. As long as you're living with that person, I don't have any money. You live there with your concubine like dogs in a kennel, you bring bastards into the world and palm them off on other people, and then you have the face to come and ask your old granny for more money. Not a penny! Not one penny!

ALFRED: Is that your last word?

GRANDMOTHER: Dogs in a kennel, dogs in a kennel!

ALFRED: Old witch.

(*Silence.*)

GRANDMOTHER: What did you say?

(*ALFRED says nothing.*)

You wouldn't dare say that again.

ALFRED: I would.

GRANDMOTHER: Go on, then.

ALFRED: Witch. Old witch.

(*His GRANDMOTHER comes up to him slowly and pinches his arm. He smiles.*)

What's that supposed to be?

GRANDMOTHER: (*Pinching him.*) You just wait, you'll feel it in a minute. There. There.

(*ALFRED, who is now beginning to feel something, shakes her off.*)

ALFRED: I don't mind human beings trying to hurt me, but not frogs.

GRANDMOTHER: (*Weeping with rage.*) Give me my money back, you great lout! I want my money, you hooligan, you thief!

(*ALFRED laughs.*)

(*Shrieking.*) Stop laughing!

(*She fetches him a blow with her walking-stick.*)

ALFRED: Ow!

GRANDMOTHER: (*Grinning with satisfaction.*) You felt that? You felt that all right, did you?

ALFRED: You witch. You old witch.

(*His GRANDMOTHER lifts her stick triumphantly.*) Don't you dare!

GRANDMOTHER: I'll do what I like, you stupid boy. I could still knock you down, you know, I could still knock anyone down. Tut, you've got another button hanging off there. How you can live with such a slovenly bitch, I...

ALFRED: (*Interrupting her.*) She's certainly not slovenly!

(*Silence.*)

GRANDMOTHER: Her mouth is far too big!

ALFRED: That's a matter of taste.

GRANDMOTHER: Just a minute, I'll sew your button on for you. (*She does so.*) What d'you need a woman for, when you've got your old granny to sew your buttons on for you? Not that you're worth looking after, taking up with a beggar-woman and having a child by her, a child!

ALFRED: These things can happen.

GRANDMOTHER: You're so thoughtless, so thoughtless!

ALFRED: You know I pulled out all the stops, there was just nothing I could do about it.

(*Silence.*)

GRANDMOTHER: Poor unfortunate devil, you are, Alfred.

ALFRED: Why?

GRANDMOTHER: Because you're always falling into the clutches of women like that...

(*Silence.*)

Listen, Alfred. If you leave your precious Marianne,
I'll lend you some money…

(*Silence.*)

ALFRED: What?

GRANDMOTHER: You heard me.

(*Silence.*)

ALFRED: How much?

GRANDMOTHER: You're still young and handsome…

(*ALFRED points at the pram.*)

ALFRED: What about that?

GRANDMOTHER: Don't worry about that. Just go away
somewhere.

(*Silence.*)

ALFRED: Where?

GRANDMOTHER: France. Everything's still going well over
there, I read it in the paper. If I were young, I'd be off to
France first thing…

Scene 6

And back in the quiet street in Vienna 8

*It's already late afternoon and the schoolgirl on the second floor
is playing Johann Strauss's waltz 'Frühlingsstimmen'. OSKAR
stands in the doorway of his shop, cleaning his fingernails with
a penknife. The CAPTAIN enters, left, and nods to OSKAR.
OSKAR bows.*

CAPTAIN: Well, I really must say, that blood-sausage yesterday. My compliments. First class.

OSKAR: Tender, wasn't it?

CAPTAIN: A poem.

(*He approaches the tobacconist's. VALERIE appears in
the doorway of the tobacconist's. The CAPTAIN greets her.
VALERIE responds.*)

May I have a look at the lottery results?

(*VALERIE gets them from the rack by the door and hands
them to him.*)

Enchanté.

(He buries himself in the list of results and the waltz ends.
The ZAUBERKÖNIG accompanies the LADY out of the
dolls' hospital.)

LADY: I bought some tin soldiers here once before, last year…
but then I was served by a very polite girl.

ZAUBERKÖNIG: *(Surly.)* Could be.

LADY: Was that your daughter?

ZAUBERKÖNIG: I have no daughter. I never had a daughter!

LADY: Pity. So, you won't order a box of tin soldiers for me?

ZAUBERKÖNIG: I explained it to you inside, ordering
things is much too much paperwork, just for one box.
Why don't you buy the little chappie something along the
same lines? Like a nice trumpet perhaps?

LADY: No. Goodbye.

(She leaves him there, annoyed, and exits.)

ZAUBERKÖNIG: *Enchanté!* Drop dead! *(He exits into the dolls'*
hospital.)

VALERIE: *(Spitefully.)* And what have we won this time,
Captain?

(ERICH comes out of the tobacconist's and tries to leave
quickly.)

VALERIE: Just a minute! What's that you've got?

ERICH: Five Memphis.

VALERIE: What again? He smokes like a grown-up.

(The CAPTAIN and OSKAR are listening.)

ERICH: *(Through his teeth.)* Look, if I don't smoke, I can't
work. And if I don't work, I'll never get to be a barrister.
And if I don't, there's hardly any chance I shall ever be in
a position to be able to pay back my debts.

VALERIE: What debts?

ERICH: You know very well. I'm scrupulous about these
things, Madame.

VALERIE: Scrupulous? Are you trying to upset me again?

ERICH: Upset you? It's a matter of honour. I pay my debts
down to the last penny, even if it takes me a hundred
years! We don't leave ourselves open to comment, you
know, it's a matter of honour! And now I must get to the
college… *(He exits.)*

VALERIE: *(Staring after him.)* Matter of honour. Pig…

(*The CAPTAIN and OSKAR grin to themselves.*)

CAPTAIN: (*Spitefully getting his own back.*) And how are things otherwise, Frau Valerie?

(*ERICH suddenly reappears.*)

ERICH: (*To the CAPTAIN.*) Did I see you smirking just now? You, sir!

VALERIE: (*Nervously.*) Do you gentlemen know each other?

CAPTAIN: By sight.

ERICH: You're an Austrian. All mouth and no guts.

VALERIE: Erich!

CAPTAIN: What did he say?

ERICH: I said the Austrians were totally spineless in the war, and if it hadn't been for us Prussians...

CAPTAIN: (*Finishing his sentence.*) ...there'd never have been a war at all!

ERICH: What about Sarajevo? What about Bosnia-Herzegovina?

CAPTAIN: What do you know about the world war, you whippersnapper? What you were taught in school, that's all.

ERICH: Well, that's better than teaching old Jewesses to play bridge!

VALERIE: Erich!

CAPTAIN: Yes, and it's better than leeching off old tobacconists!

VALERIE: Captain!

CAPTAIN: I apologise. That was a *faux pas*. A *lapsus linguae*. (*He kisses her hand.*) It was deplorable, quite deplorable. But this greenhorn has never earned himself a penny in his whole life.

ERICH: Very well, sir!

VALERIE: No, not a duel, for God's sake!

ERICH: I assume you'd be prepared to give satisfaction.

CAPTAIN: You want to take me to court?

VALERIE: Jesus, Mary and Joseph!

ERICH: I do not allow myself to be insulted!

CAPTAIN: No-one's going to insult me and get away with it! Certainly not you!

VALERIE: Please, stop it, this is a scandal…

(*She exits, sobbing, into the tobacconist's.*)

CAPTAIN: I refuse to allow these things to be said about me by this Prussian. Where were your Hohenzollerns then, when our Habsburgs were already Holy Roman Emperors, tell me that? Still in the trees!

ERICH: That is the last straw.

CAPTAIN: (*Calling after him.*) Here's twenty groschen, get yourself a haircut, you great cockatoo! (*He turns and starts to exit left, then stops again in front of the butcher's.*
To OSKAR.) By the way, I know what I meant to ask you: are you slaughtering the pig today?

OSKAR: I'm about to, captain.

CAPTAIN: Save me a nice bit of kidney, will you?

OSKAR: Be glad to, Captain.

CAPTAIN: *Enchanté.*

(*He exits, left, and upstairs the schoolgirl starts playing again, this time the waltz 'Über den Wellen'. ALFRED strolls on, left. OSKAR is about to go back into the butcher's, but catches sight of ALFRED, who doesn't notice him, and watches him secretly. ALFRED stops in front of the dolls' hospital, reminiscing. Then he moves on to the open door of the tobacconist's and stands looking in. Pause. ALFRED nods.*
Pause. After a time, VALERIE appears in the doorway, and the waltz breaks off, again in mid-phrase. Silence.)

ALFRED: Could I have five Memphis?

VALERIE: No.

(*Silence.*)

ALFRED: This is a tobacconist's, isn't it?

VALERIE: No.

(*Silence.*)

ALFRED: I just happened to be passing, by chance…

VALERIE: Oh, yes?

ALFRED: Yes.

(*Silence.*)

VALERIE: And how is the young sir?

ALFRED: So-so, you know.

VALERIE: And your young lady?

ALFRED: So-so.

VALERIE: Oh, yes?

(*Silence.*)

ALFRED: And you're all right, I hope?

VALERIE: I have everything I need.

ALFRED: Everything?

VALERIE: Everything. He's a law-student.

ALFRED: They'll take anything for lawyers nowadays.

VALERIE: What?

ALFRED: Congratulations.

(*Silence.*)

VALERIE: Where is poor Marianne?

ALFRED: I may well be losing sight of her…

(*Silence.*)

VALERIE: You really are a champion bastard, aren't you, even your worst enemy would have to give you that.

ALFRED: Valerie, he that is without sin, let him cast the first stone at me.

VALERIE: Are you ill?

ALFRED: No. Just tired. And rushed off my feet. I'm not as young as I was.

VALERIE: Since when?

ALFRED: I'm going to France this evening. Nancy. I think I might be able to find something that'll suit me better, in the haulage business. I'd have to sink too far below my own standards if I stayed here.

VALERIE: What about the gee-gees?

ALFRED: Don't ask me! Anyway, where would I find the capital…?

(*Silence.*)

VALERIE: If I get the time, I might feel sorry for you.

ALFRED: Would you like it, if things went badly for me?

VALERIE: I thought you hadn't a care in the world.

ALFRED: Would you like it, if that were true?

(*Silence.*)

I just happened to be passing through, by chance…felt a kind of melancholic nostalgia…for my old haunts…

(*He exits, and the waltz 'Über den Wellen' starts up once again.*)

VALERIE: (*Catching sight of OSKAR.*) Herr Oskar! Guess who I've just been chatting to.

OSKAR: I saw.

VALERIE: Ah. Things are going badly for them.

OSKAR: I heard.

(*Pause.*)

VALERIE: He still has the pride of a Spaniard…

OSKAR: Pride comes before a fall. Poor Marianne…

VALERIE: I should think you could still marry her, now she's on her own again…

OSKAR: Yes, if it wasn't for the child…

VALERIE: If anyone had done that to me…

OSKAR: I still love her. Perhaps the child'll die…

VALERIE: Herr Oskar!

OSKAR: Who knows? Though the mills of God grind slowly, yet they grind extremely small. I shall never forget my Marianne. I shall take all her sufferings on myself, whom the Lord loveth, He chasteneth. He scourgeth. He chastiseth. With red-hot irons and molten lead…

VALERIE: (*Shouts at him.*) Stop it, please.

(*OSKAR smiles. HAVLITSCHEK comes out of the butcher's.*)

HAVLITSCHEK: Well, what's the story? Am I going to stick the pig or am I not?

OSKAR: No, Havlitschek. I'm going to do it myself today, I'll stick the pig…

(*Peal of bells.*)

Scene 7

In St Stephen's cathedral

In front of St Anthony's side-altar. MARIANNE is at confession. The bells fall silent and all is peaceful.

CONFESSOR: To recap, then: you've caused the most agonising suffering and anxiety to your poor old father, who loves you more than anything and only ever wanted the best for you, you've been disobedient and ungrateful, you've abandoned an admirable fiancé in order to bind yourself to a degenerate, driven on by lust...be quiet! That much we've established. And now you've been living with this wretched individual outside the holy sacrament of marriage for over a year, and in this appalling state of mortal sin, you've conceived and given birth to a child. When was that?

MARIANNE: Eight weeks ago.

CONFESSOR: A child of shame and sin, and you've not even had it baptised. Now tell me: do you think anything good can come of all this? No, never! And as if that wasn't enough, you didn't even shrink from wanting to kill the child in your womb...

MARIANNE: No, that was him! I only agreed to go through with it because of him!

CONFESSOR: Only because of him?

MARIANNE: He didn't want to bring a child into the world, because times are getting worse and worse and nobody knows what's going to happen...but I...the fact I tried to have an abortion, every time the baby looks at me, I can't bear to think of it.

(*Silence.*)

CONFESSOR: Did you keep it?

MARIANNE: No.

CONFESSOR: Where is it?

MARIANNE: With relatives. Out in the Wachau.

CONFESSOR: Godfearing people?

MARIANNE: I'm sure they are.

(*Silence.*)

CONFESSOR: So you repent having wanted to kill it?

MARIANNE: Yes.

CONFESSOR: And living out of wedlock with that brute?

(*Silence.*)

MARIANNE: I thought I'd found the man who would make my life complete...

CONFESSOR: Do you repent?

(*Silence.*)

MARIANNE: Yes.

CONFESSOR: And having conceived and given birth to a child in a state of mortal sin, do you repent that too?
(*Silence.*)

MARIANNE: No. You can't...

CONFESSOR: What's that?

MARIANNE: He is my child, after all...

CONFESSOR: But you're...

MARIANNE: (*Interrupting him.*) I'm not going to. No. I'd be frightened to think I could repent that. No, I'm happy I have him, very happy...
(*Silence.*)

CONFESSOR: If you're not able to repent, what is it you expect from the Lord?

MARIANNE: I thought perhaps He would have something to tell me...

CONFESSOR: You only come to Him when things are going badly?

MARIANNE: When things are going well, I think He's with me anyway...but He can't want me to repent a thing like that...that would be completely unnatural...

CONFESSOR: Then go away! And until you can come to terms with yourself, don't appear before Our Lord again.
(*He makes the sign of the cross.*)

MARIANNE: Then I'm sorry.
(*She gets up from the confessional, now melting into darkness, and the murmur of a litany is heard. Gradually the priest's voice can be distinguished from the voices of the congregation. MARIANNE listens: the litany ends with the Lord's Prayer. MARIANNE's lips move. Silence.*)
Amen.
(*Silence.*)
If there is a God...what's to become of me, God? Dear God, I was born in Vienna Eight and I went to the local secondary school, I'm not a bad person...are you listening? What's to become of me, God?
(*Silence.*)

End of Act Two.

ACT THREE

Scene 1

At the tavern

Tavern music and falling blossom. Bibulous atmosphere. And, in the thick of it, the ZAUBERKÖNIG, VALERIE and ERICH. Everyone is singing:

ALL: *Da draussen in der Wachau*
    Die Donau fliesst so blau,
    Steht einsam ein Winzerhaus,
    Da schaut ein Mädel heraus.
    Hat Lippen rot wie Blut,
    Und küssen kanns so gut,
    Die Augen sind veilchenblau
    Vom Mädel in der Wachau.

    Es wird ein Wein sein,
    Und wir werden nimmer sein.
    Es wird schöne Madeln geben,
    Und wir werden nimmer leben...

    (Now, for a moment, a deathly hush falls on the tavern... then everyone starts singing again, three times as loud.)

    Drum gehn wir gern nach Nussdorf naus,
    Da gibts a Hetz, a Gstanz,
    Da hörn wir ferme Tanz,
    Da lass ma fesche Jodler naus
    Und gengan in der Fruah
    Mitn Schwomma zhaus, mitn Schwomma zhaus!

    (Enthusiastic applause. Between the tables, people start dancing to the 'Radetsky March'. By now everyone is well away.)
ZAUBERKÖNIG: Bravo, bravissimo! I'm my old self today!
    Da capo, da capo! (He grabs at a GIRL's breasts as she dances by. Her BOYFRIEND slaps his hand.)

BOYFRIEND: Hands off the tits!

GIRL: They're my tits.

ZAUBERKÖNIG: What's a tit between friends? Everyone has his troubles, but today I want to forget them all! I don't give a bugger for anything!

ERICH: Listen, everybody! I hereby propose a most lavish toast to the famous Viennese wine festival. Cheers!
(*He spills his wine.*)

VALERIE: Don't get so worked up, boy! My God, it's spilt all over me.

ERICH: Accidents will happen. It's a matter of honour.

ZAUBERKÖNIG: Has he made you wet? You poor wee thing.

VALERIE: Soaked to the skin.

ZAUBERKÖNIG: To the skin, eh...

VALERIE: Now, don't be cheeky.

ERICH: Attention!
(*He clicks his heels and stands to attention.*)

ZAUBERKÖNIG: What's the matter with him?

VALERIE: I'm used to it now. When he's plastered, he gives himself orders all the time.

ZAUBERKÖNIG: He's very good at it. Straight. Really straight. Bit of respect. We're on the way up again.
(*He collapses under the table.*)

VALERIE: Jesus!

ZAUBERKÖNIG: This chair is broken. Waiter, another chair! Hey, another chair! (*He sings along with the music.*) *Ach, ich hab sie ja nur auf die Schulter geküsst...und schon hab ich den Patsch verspürt mit dem Fächer ins Gesicht...*
(*A WAITER brings a gigantic portion of salami.*)

VALERIE: Salami, Erich! Salami!

ERICH: Company! Stand at ease!
(*He reaches into the bowl and starts guzzling at an alarming rate.*)

ZAUBERKÖNIG: The way he shovels it in!

VALERIE: *Bon appétit.*

ZAUBERKÖNIG: Don't be so greedy!

VALERIE: One thing, he's not paying.

ZAUBERKÖNIG: And he can't even sing.

(*Pause.*)

VALERIE: (*To ERICH.*) Why won't you sing?

ERICH: (*With his mouth full.*) Because of my chronic sore throat.

VALERIE: You smoke too much.

ERICH: (*Yelling at her.*) Don't start that again!

(*The CAPTAIN appears, wearing a little paper hat and in high spirits.*)

CAPTAIN: *Enchanté,* my dear Frau Valerie. What a pleasant surprise! Greetings, Herr Zauberkönig!

ZAUBERKÖNIG: *Prost,* Captain, my dear Captain, *Prost!*

(*He empties his glass, and lapses into a melancholy stupor.*)

VALERIE: May I offer you some of my salami, Captain?

(*ERICH stops in mid-chew and glares at the CAPTAIN with hatred.*)

CAPTAIN: Too kind, *enchanté.* But no, I couldn't possibly fit any more... (*He sticks two thick slices into his mouth.*) I've had two lots of dinner already this evening, I've got a visitor... I've been sitting over there with him. He's a school friend of my brother who went missing in Siberia: an American.

VALERIE: Ah, a Yank.

CAPTAIN: Born in Vienna, though. He's been over there in the States for twenty years, and this is his first time back in Europe. This morning when we drove through the Hofburg, he had tears in his eyes. He's what they call a self-made man. Does everything for himself.

VALERIE: Oo, you are dreadful!

CAPTAIN: Yes. And I'm showing him round his Vienna. This is the second day. I'm afraid we'll never be sober again.

VALERIE: Still waters run deep.

CAPTAIN: Yes, and not only in America.

ERICH: (*Aggressively.*) Oh, really?

(*Pause.*)

VALERIE: (*Approaching ERICH.*) Behave yourself. And shut up or I'll clout you. If you're going to scoff all my salami, I want a bit of consideration.

ERICH: That kind of remark is a tribute to your mean-mindedness, Madame.

VALERIE: Stop it!

ERICH: Attention! Company…

VALERIE: Halt!

ERICH: Company, by the left, quick march!
(*He exits.*)

VALERIE: (*Calling after him.*) About turn! About turn!
(*Deathly silence.*)

CAPTAIN: Who is that, anyway?

VALERIE: (*Tonelessly.*) He thinks he's a whole army. Soon I'm
going to leave him flat. I can see it coming. (*She points to the
ZAUBERKÖNIG.*) He's a distant relation of that one.
(*The music starts up again.*)

CAPTAIN: Speaking of relations, tell me, Frau Valerie, do you
think it's right the way His Majesty Herr Zauberkönig has
treated Fräulein Marianne? I can't understand it. If I was a
grandfather… I mean, anyway, it's easy to make a mistake.
But just to let things go like that…

VALERIE: Have you heard any more details, Captain?

CAPTAIN: I once had a colonel's wife, that's to say, the whole
regiment had her…what am I talking about?
I mean, she was the colonel's wife, and the colonel had
an illegitimate child by some girl from the music hall, but
his wife took it in as if it were her own flesh and blood,
because, you see, she was barren. Now, when you look
at the way old Zauberkönig over there has behaved,
compared to that…well, say no more.

VALERIE: I don't understand, Captain. What's the colonel's
wife got to do with Marianne?

CAPTAIN: People don't understand each other any more,
Frau Valerie. Quite often we don't understand ourselves.

VALERIE: Where is Marianne?

CAPTAIN: (*Smiling mysteriously.*) There will be an official
announcement about that, when the time is ripe.
(*The AMERICAN appears: he is drunk.*)

AMERICAN: My dear old friend…what's this I see? People?
Friends? Introduce me, will you please? Dear old friend…
(*He embraces the CAPTAIN. The ZAUBERKÖNIG
awakes from his stupor.*)

ZAUBERKÖNIG: Who's that?

CAPTAIN: This is my friend from America.

AMERICAN: America! New York! Chicago! Sing Sing! That's just on the outside: inside beats the old honest to God real golden Viennese heart, eternal Vienna...and the Wachau... and the castles by the blue Danube. (*He hums along to the music.*) Donau so blau, so blau, so blau...
(*Everyone joins in, swaying in their seats.*)
Ladies and gentlemen, there's been a lot of changes lately, there's been storms and whirlwinds all over the world, and earthquakes and tornadoes, and I had to start right from the bottom, but I'm right at home here, I know my way round here, I like it here, I want to die here! With the Lord God of old Austria from Mariazell!
(*He sings.*)
Mein Muatterl war a Weanerin,
Drum hab ich Wean so gern.
Sie wars, die mit dem Leben
Mir die Liebe hat gegeben
Zu meinem anzigen goldenen Wean!
(*Everyone sings.*)

ALL: *Wien, Wien, nur du allein*
Sollst stets die Stadt meiner Träume sein,
Dort, wo ich glücklich und selig bin,
Ist Wien, ist Wien, mein Wien!

AMERICAN: Long live Vienna! Home! And the beautiful Viennese women! And all the memories of home! And long live the Viennese, all of us, every one, every one.

ALL: Vienna!
(*Everybody drinks.*)

ZAUBERKÖNIG: (*To VALERIE.*) And the beautiful Viennese women, you magnificent creature. I should have married you, with you I would've had a quite different child.

VALERIE: I wish you wouldn't keep talking about Irene. I could never stand her.

AMERICAN: Who's Irene?

ZAUBERKÖNIG: Irene was my wife.

AMERICAN: Oh, pardon me.

ZAUBERKÖNIG: That's all right. Why shouldn't I complain about Irene? Just because she's dead? She ruined my whole life.

VALERIE: You're a devil.

ZAUBERKÖNIG: (*Sings.*)
Mir ist mei Alte gstorbn,
Drum ist mirs Herz so schwer.
A so a gute Seel
Krieg ich nöt mehr,
Muss so viel wana,
Das glaubt mir kana,
Dass ich mich kränk,
Wenn ich an mei Alte denk! Olé!

AMERICAN: (*Jumping up.*) Olé! Olé! Unless I'm very much mistaken, it's starting to rain. But we're not going to let the weather get in our way. Tonight we're going to take it easy, let the rain pitter-patter, but it really doesn't matter.
(*He shakes a finger at the sky.*) You want to rain, do you? Rest of the evening's on me. You're all invited! Every one of you!
(*Enthusiastic response from everyone.*)
Okay. Off we go. Follow me!

VALERIE: Where to?

AMERICAN: Anywhere! Anywhere with a ceiling! So's we don't have to sit out in the open. The *Moulin Bleu*!
(*Loud applause.*)

CAPTAIN: Wait! Not the *Moulin Bleu*, my friends. Let's go to Maxim's!
(*Again, for a moment, a deathly silence.*)

ZAUBERKÖNIG: Why Maxim's?

CAPTAIN: Because there's a very special surprise waiting for us there.

ZAUBERKÖNIG: What kind of a surprise?

CAPTAIN: Something spicy. Very spicy.
(*Silence.*)

ZAUBERKÖNIG: Alright, Maxim's it is.

ALL: Maxim's.
(*They march off with raised umbrellas, singing.*)

Vindobona, du herrliche Stadt,
Die so reizende Anlagen hat,
Dir gehört stets nur unser Sinn.
Ja zu dir, da ziagts uns hin,
San ma a von dir oft fern,
Denkn ma do ans liebe Wean,
Denn du bleibst die Perle von Österreich,
Dir ist gar ka Stadt net gleich!

Die Mizzi und der Jean
Gehn Miteinander drahn,
Wir sind ja nicht aus Stroh,
Sind jung und lebensfroh,
Net immer Schokoladi,
Heut gehen wir zum 'Brady'
Oder zum 'Maxim'
Heut sind wir einmal schlimm!

Jetzt trink ma noch a Flascherl Wein,
Hollodero!
Es muss ja nöt das letzte sein
Hollodero!
Und ist das gar, gibts ka Geniern,
Hollodero!
So tun wir noch mal repetiern, aber noch mal repetiern!
(Gong. The stage is transformed into Maxim's. A bar and
private booths. In the background a cabaret stage with a
wide ramp. They all close their umbrellas and sit at the
tables in the most expansive mood. The COMPÈRE steps
out in front of the curtain.)

COMPÈRE: Honoured guests, ladies and gentlemen!
Delightful ladies and even more delightful gentlemen!

VALERIE: Aha!

(Laughter.)

COMPÈRE: I bid you a most hearty welcome on behalf of the
management! As Johann Wolfgang von Goethe, the prince
of poets, says in his masterpiece the immortal *Faust*: 'That
which thy father bequeathed thee, earn it anew, if thou
wouldst possess it.' In other words, ladies and gentlemen,
we expect you all to join in the songs. That's the tradition

of the house, ladies and gentlemen. And now, I want you
to come with us down memory lane!

(*The orchestra strikes up Johann Strauss's waltz 'Wiener
Blut', the curtain goes up, and girls in Old Vienna costumes
dance the waltz. Then the curtain falls. Tremendous
enthusiasm from the audience and the orchestra plays the
'Hoch-und Deutschmeister March'.*)

ZAUBERKÖNIG: (*To the CAPTAIN.*) What are you talking
about? It's been established beyond the shadow of a doubt
that we're descended from the animals.

CAPTAIN: It's open to debate.

ZAUBERKÖNIG: I suppose you believe in Adam and Eve.

CAPTAIN: Who knows?

AMERICAN: (*To VALERIE.*) You bobcat!

ZAUBERKÖNIG: Bobcat! Or a leopard maybe.

VALERIE: *Prost*, Zauberkönig!

ZAUBERKÖNIG: The captain is some fabulous beast, you
have something of the kangaroo in you, and the Yank is a
Japanese pug.

AMERICAN: (*Not laughing at all.*) You're a thousand laughs.

ZAUBERKÖNIG: And what about me?

VALERIE: You're a stag. An old stag. *Prost*, old stag!
(*Roars of laughter. The table telephone rings. Silence.*)

ZAUBERKÖNIG: (*Answering.*) Hello, yes?… What? Who's
that? Mousey?… Mousey, never heard of you. What?…
Oh, I see, yes, that's right, that's right, I'm your uncle…
What do you want? Oo, you devil, you little piggie…
Where? At the bar? In the green dress?… What? You're
still a virgin? You expect your old uncle to believe that?
Well, I shall have to check, won't I?…
(*He makes kissing sounds, hangs up and empties the glass
of champagne the AMERICAN has ordered.*)

VALERIE: You shouldn't drink so much, Leopold.

ZAUBERKÖNIG: Take a running jump. (*He gets up.*) When
you're as old as I am, alcohol's the only pleasure left.
Where's the bar?

VALERIE: What bar?

ZAUBERKÖNIG: The bar, for Christ's sake!

CAPTAIN: I'll take you.

ZAUBERKÖNIG: I can find it myself, I don't need a guide dog! Come on then, show me!

(*He lets the CAPTAIN lead him to the bar, where two girls are waiting for him. The one in the green dress gives him a warm welcome. The CAPTAIN stays by the bar as well.*)

AMERICAN: (*To VALERIE.*) What does he do?

VALERIE: Runs a toyshop.

AMERICAN: Oh.

VALERIE: Yes. Apart from that, he's a bit of a rarity, modest and respectable, a real representative of the old school. It's a dying breed.

AMERICAN: Pity.

VALERIE: Unfortunately, he's plastered today…

AMERICAN: The way you said that. What charm! Back in the States, everything's so much more brutal.

VALERIE: How much do you weigh?

AMERICAN: Two hundred eighteen pounds.

VALERIE: My God!

AMERICAN: May I speak frankly?

VALERIE: Please do.

AMERICAN: I'm complicated.

VALERIE: How do you mean?

AMERICAN: I mean, inside, I'm dead. It's got so's I can only make out with prostitutes. That's because of the many disappointments in my past.

VALERIE: Who'd have thought it? Such a sensitive soul in such a huge body…

AMERICAN: I was born under Saturn.

VALERIE: Yes, those old stars! We're stuck with them and there's nothing we can do about it.

(*Gong. The COMPÈRE steps out in front of the curtain.*)

COMPÈRE: And now, ladies and gentlemen, once again we have for you a wonderful act. I won't waste words describing it, judge for yourselves our sensational, highly artistic, and specially designed for us by the most distinguished artists: our *tableaux vivants*. And first, the Mermaids of the Danube: Maestro, if you please!

(*The orchestra strikes up with 'The Blue Danube Waltz'
and the house lights go out. Then the curtains open to
reveal three half-naked girls, legs encased in tail-fins. One
holds a lyre. They are picturesquely grouped in front of
a black curtain lit by green spotlights. From the bar, the
ZAUBERKÖNIG's voice is heard.*)

ZAUBERKÖNIG: Naked women, I should think so too!

(*The curtains close to loud applause. Gong. The
COMPÈRE appears in front of the curtain again.*)

COMPÈRE: The second tableau: the Zeppelin!

(*Cheers.*)

Maestro, if you please!

(*Now the 'Fredericus Rex' is played, and three naked girls
are standing on the stage. The first holds a propeller in her
hands, the second a globe and the third a small zeppelin.
Tumultuous applause from the audience, who jump up from
their seats and sing the first verse of 'Deutschland Über
Alles', after which silence falls. Gong. The COMPÈRE,
in front of the curtain again.*)

And now, ladies and gentlemen, the third tableau:
'The Search for Happiness'.

(*Deathly silence.*)

Maestro, if you please!

(*Schumann's 'Reverie', and the curtains open for the third
time. A group of naked girls are trampling each other down,
trying to run after a golden sphere, on which Happiness
is balancing on one leg. Happiness is equally naked and
is MARIANNE. VALERIE cries out shrilly in the dark
auditorium.*)

VALERIE: Marianne! Jesus, Mary and Joseph! Marianne!

(*MARIANNE, shocked, starts to wobble on her sphere, can't
keep her balance, has to step down, and stares, blinded by
the spotlights, into the dark auditorium.*)

AMERICAN: What's the matter?

VALERIE: (*Beside herself.*) Marianne, Marianne, Marianne!

AMERICAN: (*Getting furious.*) Will you stop shouting!

Are you nuts?

VALERIE: Marianne!

AMERICAN: Shut up! I'll give you Marianne!

(*He punches her in the breast. VALERIE screams. Uproar in the audience. Shouts of 'Lights! Lights!' The COMPÈRE rushes on to the stage.*)

COMPÈRE: Curtain! What's going on? Lights! Curtain! Lights!

(*The curtain falls in front of MARIANNE, who is still staring out into the auditorium, the other girls having already exited in confusion. The house-lights come up and again, for a moment, there falls a deathly hush. Everyone is staring at VALERIE, who is sitting, slumped, face down on the table, hysterical and drunk, weeping and sobbing. The ZAUBERKÖNIG is standing at the bar, his hand on his heart.*)

VALERIE: (*Whimpering.*) Marianne… Marianne…dear little Marianne… Oh, oh, oh… I knew her when she was five years old!

COMPÈRE: What's she talking about?

AMERICAN: Search me.

COMPÈRE: Hysterical?

AMERICAN: Epileptic.

A FRIENDLY VOICE: Throw her out, drunken cow!

VALERIE: I'm not drunk. That's one thing I'm not. I'm not, I'm not! (*She jumps up, intending to run out, but trips over her own feet and falls, knocking a table over as she does so and cutting herself.*) I can't, I can't stand it, I'm not made of stone, I'm still full of life… I can't stand it, I can't stand it!

(*She rushes out, bawling. Everyone, except for the ZAUBERKÖNIG, watches her go, bewildered. Silence, then the gong. The COMPÈRE gets up on a chair.*)

COMPÈRE: Honoured guests! Ladies and gentlemen! That concludes the official part of tonight's programme…the unofficial part is about to commence in the bar!

(*Dance music starts up in the bar.*)

On behalf of the management, I should like to thank you for turning up in such numbers and wish you a very good night. Good night, ladies and gentlemen.

(*The clientèle gradually disperses from the club.*)

ZAUBERKÖNIG: Captain...

CAPTAIN: Yes?

ZAUBERKÖNIG: So that's why you wanted to come here instead of the *Moulin Bleu*. That was the spicy surprise you were talking about, I had a funny feeling when you said that, I had a suspicion it wouldn't be anything good...

CAPTAIN: I knew Fräulein Marianne was appearing here. I come here quite often, I was here yesterday, and I can't just be a spectator any more. If you weren't so hard-hearted...

ZAUBERKÖNIG: Don't interfere in family matters which are no business of yours, soldier!

CAPTAIN: I considered it my human duty...

ZAUBERKÖNIG: (*Interrupting him.*) What's that?

CAPTAIN: You're just not human!

ZAUBERKÖNIG: Oh, that's nice! That's very nice! What am I then, if I'm not human, mm? Perhaps I'm a cow? Would that suit you? Well, I'm not a cow and I don't have a daughter either, do you understand?

CAPTAIN: Well, I've nothing more to do here.

(*He bows stiffly and exits.*)

ZAUBERKÖNIG: And what am I supposed to do here? You bastard! I feel as if this is the end, Mr American. I better write some postcards, so's everyone'll drop dead with envy, when they hear what a wonderful time I'm having.

AMERICAN: Postcards! Terrific idea! What an idea! Postcards!

(*He buys a whole pile from a salesgirl, sits at a table some way away and starts writing. He's alone now with the ZAUBERKÖNIG. The sound of dance music from the bar. MARIANNE enters slowly in a bathrobe and stops in front of the ZAUBERKÖNIG. The ZAUBERKÖNIG stares at her, looks her up and down, then turns his back on her. Pause.*)

MARIANNE: Why didn't you read my letters? I wrote to you three times. You sent them back without opening them.

(*Pause.*)

I wrote and told you he'd left me...

(*The ZAUBERKÖNIG turns to her slowly and stares at her with hatred.*)

ZAUBERKÖNIG: I know that.

(*He turns his back on her again. Pause.*)

MARIANNE: And did you also know I have a child...?

ZAUBERKÖNIG: Of course.

(*Pause.*)

MARIANNE: We're having a hard time, little Leopold and I...

ZAUBERKÖNIG: What? Leopold? I'm Leopold! This is the limit! Calling your shame after me! On top of everything else! Well, that's the end! You never listened to me, now you'll have to take the consequences. That's the end!

(*He gets up, but has to sit down again.*)

MARIANNE: You're drunk, Papa...

ZAUBERKÖNIG: Don't be so vulgar! And once and for all, I'm not your papa! And don't be vulgar, or I'll...

(*He threatens to slap her face.*) You'd do better to think about your mother! The dead see everything!

MARIANNE: If my mother was still alive...

ZAUBERKÖNIG: You leave your mother out of it, do you hear! If she'd seen you standing around naked on the stage, showing yourself off to everybody... Have you no shame? My God!

MARIANNE: No, I can't afford shame.

(*Silence. The music in the bar has stopped.*)

I earn two schillings a day here. It's not much, when you consider little Leopold. But what else is there for me to do? You never let me learn anything, not even eurhythmics, you brought me up to get married...

ZAUBERKÖNIG: You miserable wretch! Now it's my fault!

MARIANNE: Listen, Papa...

ZAUBERKÖNIG: (*Interrupting her.*) I am not your papa!

(*MARIANNE bangs the table with her fist.*)

MARIANNE: Shut up! If you're not my papa, who is? Now, listen to me, will you? If I lose this job, I've no way of earning anything. I can't go on the game, I can't, I've tried it, but I just can't give myself to a man, unless I love him with all my heart. I'm an uneducated woman, there's nothing else I have to offer...all that's left for me is the train.

ZAUBERKÖNIG: What train?

MARIANNE: The train. The train you travel on. I'm going to throw myself in front of it...

ZAUBERKÖNIG: I see. That as well. You'd do that to me as well. (*He bursts into tears.*) You filthy slut, what are you trying to do to my old age? It's one disgrace after another. I'm just a poor old man, what have I done to deserve this?

MARIANNE: (*Sharply.*) Stop thinking about yourself the whole time!

(*The ZAUBERKÖNIG stops crying, and stares at her, furious.*)

ZAUBERKÖNIG: Alright, throw yourself in front of the train! Go on, throw yourself in front of it and take your brat with you!... I don't feel well, I don't... I wish I could be sick... (*He bends forward over the table, straightens up suddenly.*) You'd better think about God, you'd better think about your Father up there in Heaven...

(*He staggers off. MARIANNE watches him go then looks up towards Heaven.*)

MARIANNE: (*Quietly.*) In Heaven...

(*Dance music starts up again in the bar. The AMERICAN has finished writing his postcards and notices MARIANNE, who is still looking up to Heaven.*)

AMERICAN: Aha, a dame. (*He watches her, smiling.*) Say, you haven't by any chance got a stamp on you?

MARIANNE: No.

AMERICAN: (*Slowly.*) Only I need two schillings worth of stamps and I'm paying fifty schillings for them.
(*Pause.*)
Sixty schillings.
(*Pause. He takes out his wallet.*)

AMERICAN: Those are the schillings and those are the dollars.

MARIANNE: Show me.
(*The AMERICAN hands her the wallet. Pause.*)
Sixty?

AMERICAN: Sixty-five.

MARIANNE: That's a lot of money.

AMERICAN: It'll be earned.

(*Silence. The dance music has stopped again.*)

MARIANNE: No. Thank you.

(*She gives him back the wallet.*)

AMERICAN: What do you mean?

MARIANNE: I can't. You've made a mistake, sir...

(*The AMERICAN suddenly grabs her wrist and bellows.*)

AMERICAN: Stop! Stop, you've stolen my money, you tart,
you thief, you criminal, open your hand, open it!

MARIANNE: Ow!

AMERICAN: There! A hundred schillings! Did you think
I wouldn't notice, you stupid whore? (*He slaps her face.*)
Police! Police!

(*Everyone appears from the bar.*)

COMPÈRE: For Christ's sake, now what's the matter?

AMERICAN: This whore has stolen my money. A hundred
schillings, a hundred schillings! Police!

(*MARIANNE struggles free from the AMERICAN.*)

MARIANNE: You're not to hit me again. I won't be hit again!

(*The BARONESS appears. MARIANNE cries out in terror.*)

Scene 2

Out in the Wachau

*ALFRED sits with his GRANDMOTHER in front of the cottage
in the evening sun. Not far off is the pram.*

GRANDMOTHER: I always knew you were a liar, but
I never in my wildest dreams realised what a shit you are.
You borrow three hundred schillings off me to go and work
for a haulage firm in France, and after three weeks you
come back and confess you've never even been to France,
and you've gambled it all away at the races! You'll finish up
alongside that fine Marianne of yours. In gaol!

ALFRED: For one thing she's not in gaol, she's on remand,
and her trial doesn't come up till tomorrow. Also it was
only attempted theft, no harm came to anyone, there are
mitigating circumstances and they're bound to give her a
suspended sentence, she has no previous convictions...

GRANDMOTHER: That's right, stick up for her, stick up for her. You've made a proper fool of me, I knew all along you were a criminal.

ALFRED: Won't you forgive me, then?

GRANDMOTHER: Go to hell!

ALFRED: Yah!

(*He sticks his tongue out.*)

GRANDMOTHER: Yah!

(*She sticks her tongue out at him. Silence.*)

ALFRED: (*Getting up.*) Well, you won't be seeing me for a good long time.

GRANDMOTHER: What about my three hundred schillings? And the hundred and fifty I lent you last year?

ALFRED: I don't care how furious it makes you, but to some extent I can't help feeling responsible for what's happened to Marianne.

(*GRANDMOTHER gasps for breath. ALFRED raises his straw hat.*)

Enchanté, Granny. (*He exits.*)

GRANDMOTHER: (*Beside herself with rage.*) And mind you don't come back! Mucky bastard! How dare you speak to me like that? Go on, get out of here, you shit!

(*She sits at the table on which her zither is lying and tunes it. Alfred's MOTHER comes out of the cottage.*)

MOTHER: Has Alfred gone already?

GRANDMOTHER: Yes, thank God!

MOTHER: He didn't even say goodbye…

GRANDMOTHER: That's a fine son you've got there, insolent and idle! Just like his father.

MOTHER: Leave my husband alone! He's been in his grave ten years now and you still won't leave him alone.

GRANDMOTHER: Yes, and what put him in his grave so soon, I'd like to know. Me, I suppose? Or was it his precious alcohol? He pissed away your whole dowry.

MOTHER: I don't want to hear any more, that's enough!

GRANDMOTHER: Then shut up!

(*She plays the 'Doppeladler March' on her zither. MOTHER bends anxiously over the pram and GRANDMOTHER ends her march.*)

MOTHER: I'm worried about Leopold, he's got such a
    bad cough, and now his cheeks are all red and he looks
    quite different…just like the way it started with poor little
    Ludwig…

GRANDMOTHER: The Lord giveth and the Lord
    taketh away.

MOTHER: Mama!

GRANDMOTHER: Its mother in gaol and its father a
    layabout. It'd be better for a lot of people if it wasn't here
    any more.

MOTHER: How would you like it if you weren't here
    any more?

GRANDMOTHER: (*Shrieking.*) Don't you compare me with
    that thing! (*She points at the pram.*) My parents were decent
    people!
    (*She plays a minuet, furious.*)

MOTHER: Will you stop that!

GRANDMOTHER: There's no need to shout! Have you
    gone mad?
    (*They stare at one another. Silence.*)

MOTHER: (*Frightened.*) Mama… I saw you…

GRANDMOTHER: What?

MOTHER: I saw you last night…
    (*Silence.*)

GRANDMOTHER: (*Warily.*) What do you mean?

MOTHER: You opened both the windows and moved Le-
    opold's cot into the draught.

GRANDMOTHER: (*Shrieking.*) You dreamt it! You dreamt it!

MOTHER: No, I didn't dream it. And I don't care how
    furious you get.

Scene 3

And once again in the quiet street in Vienna 8

*The CAPTAIN is reading the list of lottery results again and
VALERIE is standing in the doorway of her tobacconist's.
Everything seems the same as ever, except that in the window of
the dolls' hospital, there's a sign saying:* 'Clearance Sale'.

VALERIE: (*Maliciously.*) And what have we won then, Captain?
(*The CAPTAIN hands her back the list.*)

CAPTAIN: It's Saturday, Frau Valerie. And tomorrow's Sunday.

VALERIE: That's life, Captain, that's the human condition.

CAPTAIN: Clearance sale! My conscience is clear, but
all the same. My motives were entirely altruistic that
time in Maxim's. A reconciliation was what I wanted,
a reconciliation. And because of that, it's just been one
tragedy after another. Poor Marianne locked up and
sentenced…

VALERIE: (*Interrupting him.*) Only a suspended sentence,
Captain.
(*Silence.*)

CAPTAIN: Is he really still angry with me, Herr Zauberkönig?

VALERIE: Why should he be?

CAPTAIN: Well, I mean, because of the terrible position
I put him in at Maxim's.

VALERIE: But, Captain, after all the things that man's been
through, he doesn't want to be angry with you more.
He's got much more forgiving, he's a broken man. The
other day, when he heard Marianne was a thief, he practically had a stroke!

CAPTAIN: It's no joke, a heart attack.

VALERIE: He heard the music of the spheres.

CAPTAIN: What do you mean, the music of the spheres?

VALERIE: When someone's very close to death, the soul
starts to leave the body, only half the soul, I mean, and it
flies away, up higher and higher, and up there there's a
strange melody playing, and that's the music of
the spheres.
(*Silence.*)

CAPTAIN: I suppose it's possible. Theoretically.
(*The schoolgirl on the second floor starts to play a Johann
Strauss waltz.*)

VALERIE: Can you keep a secret, Captain?

CAPTAIN: Of course.

VALERIE: Promise?

CAPTAIN: Well, I should think an old officer could keep
a secret. Just think of all the military secrets I know.

(*Pause.*)

VALERIE: Captain. She's been to see me.

CAPTAIN: Who?

VALERIE: Marianne. That's right, Marianne. She came looking for me. Four weeks she'd been in custody and she had nothing left but her pride, although she still had that. Until I got rid of it for her, that is, and I can tell you, I got rid of it all right. Just leave it to me, Captain, I'll get her and her papa back together again, we women understand how to fix these things much better than men. What you tried to do in Maxim's was much too direct...my God, it gave me a fright, I can tell you!

CAPTAIN: All's well that ends well.

(*ERICH enters quickly, right. He's on his way to the dolls' hospital, but spots the CAPTAIN and glares at him. The schoolgirl breaks off the waltz in mid-phrase. The CAPTAIN looks contemptuously at ERICH, then bows politely to VALERIE and exits, passing close by ERICH. ERICH watches him go, balefully, then looks at VALERIE. VALERIE starts to exit into the tobacconist's.*)

ERICH: Wait! One moment, dear lady. I just wanted to draw your attention to the fact that we shall probably never see each other again...

VALERIE: Good!

ERICH: I'm leaving first thing tomorrow. For ever.

VALERIE: *Bon voyage!*

ERICH: Thank you.

(*He bows formally, then starts off towards the doll's hospital.*)

VALERIE: (*Suddenly.*) Stop!

ERICH: As you were.

(*Silence.*)

VALERIE: We ought not to say good-bye like this. Come on, let's shake hands. Let's part good friends.

ERICH: Alright. (*He shakes hands with her, then takes a notebook out of his pocket and leafs through it.*) It's all down in black and white. Debit and credit. Every single cigarette.

VALERIE: (*Amiably.*) I don't want your cigarettes...

ERICH: It's a matter of honour!

(*VALERIE takes the hand holding the notebook and strokes it.*)

VALERIE: You're no psychologist, Erich…

(*She gives him a friendly nod and slowly exits into the tobacconist's. The schoolgirl starts playing again. ERICH watches her go. He's alone.*)

ERICH: Fifty-year-old decaying piece of shit…

(*He exits into the dolls' hospital. OSKAR comes out of the butcher's with ALFRED.*)

OSKAR: Well, in any case, thanks very much for coming to see me…and for being so agreeable *apropos* Marianne.

ALFRED: Just let's leave it at that. I renounce all claims on her. For good. (*He notices the sign in window of the dolls' hospital.*) What's that? Clearance sale?

OSKAR: (*Smiles.*) Yes, that as well, my friend. Soon there'll be no magic round here any more, that's to say, unless there's a reconciliation with our Marianne, because the old man just can't manage it on his own any more…

ALFRED: How sad it all is. Believe me, it's really not my fault, everything that's happened. When I think about it now, I can't understand it, I had it so good in those days, no problems, no worries. And then to be so careless as to let myself get mixed up in an adventure like that. It serves me right, God knows what got into me.

OSKAR: I think it was true love.

ALFRED: Oh no, I've got no talent for that. I was too kind-hearted, that's all. I just can't say no, and if you can't say no, a relationship like that's automatically going to go from bad to worse. You see, at the time, I really didn't want to break up your engagement, but with a girl like Marianne, it's got to be all or nothing, she insisted. You understand what I mean?

OSKAR: Of course. It's only on the surface the man seems to play the active part and the woman the passive. If you look into it a bit more closely…

ALFRED: You can see the abyss opening.

OSKAR: See, that's why I never really had anything against you personally, I never wished you any harm…whereas Marianne… (*He smiles.*) She's had to pay a bitter price, all right, poor thing, for the grand passion of her life…

ALFRED: Making so many people unhappy like that, it's terrible. Honestly, we men ought to stick together more.

OSKAR: We're too naive, if you ask me.

ALFRED: You said it.

(*The schoolgirl breaks off again.*)

Oskar, I don't know how to thank you for promising to help me and Valerie get back together again...

OSKAR: (*Interrupting him.*) Ssh!

(*The ZAUBERKÖNIG comes out of the dolls' hospital with ERICH. Neither of them notices ALFRED or OSKAR, who draw back into the doorway of the butcher's.*)

ZAUBERKÖNIG: Don't forget, have a good trip, Erich! Take care and safe journey to Dessau!

ERICH: Kassel, Uncle.

ZAUBERKÖNIG: Kassel, Dessau, I'll never learn. And don't forget our Vienna and your poor old uncle!

(*ERICH clicks his heels again, bows stiffly and exits without looking back. The ZAUBERKÖNIG watches him go, moved, then notices VALERIE, who, hearing ERICH's voice, has appeared in her doorway again to listen.*)

One of the best, eh?

(*The schoolgirl starts playing again. VALERIE slowly nods in agreement. The ZAUBERKÖNIG picks up a newspaper from the rack in front of the tobacconist's and leafs through it.*)

Yes, yes, Europe has to unite, because the next war'll be the end of all of us. But how are we supposed to put up with all this? I mean, what do the Czechs think they're up to? I'm telling you now: very soon there's going to be another war. There just has to be: There'll always be wars.

VALERIE: (*Still elsewhere.*) True. But that would mean the end of our civilisation as we know it.

ZAUBERKÖNIG: Civilisation or no civilisation, war's a law of nature. Just like competition in business. I mean, personally, I've got no competition, because I'm a specialised trade. And even so, I'm ruined. I just can't manage on my own any more, every customer I get makes me nervous. Before, I had my wife, and when she started to get ill, Marianne was already old enough...

VALERIE: How old?

ZAUBERKÖNIG: Old enough!

(*Pause.*)

VALERIE: If I were a grandfather…

ZAUBERKÖNIG: (*Interrupting her.*) But I'm not a grandfather, if you don't mind! (*He clutches his heart.*
The waltz breaks off.) You mustn't get me excited! Ow, my heart…

(*Silence.*)

VALERIE: Does it hurt?

ZAUBERKÖNIG: Like hell. And you know what the doctor said. I could have a heart attack just like that.

VALERIE: I remember that from my poor husband. Shooting pains, is it?

ZAUBERKOHIG: Shooting pains, that's right…

(*Silence.*)

VALERIE: Leopold. God has given you a sign. And what it is is that you're still alive. Now, calm down, don't get excited, don't get excited! Otherwise you'll have a heart attack, and if you have a heart attack, then what? You silly old buffer, the best thing to do is forgive and forget. Forgive and forget, and you'll be able to carry on your business and everything will be all right, everything, everything!

(*Silence.*)

ZAUBERKÖNIG: You think so?

VALERIE: Look, Marianne, she's not a bad person, she's just a stupid little woman. Just a poor stupid little woman.

ZAUBERKÖNIG: She's stupid all right. Thick as pigshit.

VALERIE: And she thought she could change the world the way she wanted it to be. But I'm afraid the world behaves according to reason, isn't that right, Grandpa?

ZAUBERKÖNIG: Grandpa?

VALERIE: Yes.

(*Silence. The schoolgirl starts playing again. The ZAUBERKÖNIG moves off slowly towards the dolls' hospital, stops in front of the window and looks at the clearance sale sign. Then he gives VALERIE a friendly nod, tears up the sign and vanishes into the dolls' hospital. VALERIE grins with satisfaction and lights a cigarette.*)

OSKAR: Frau Valerie! I have a surprise for you.

VALERIE: What sort of a surprise?

OSKAR: Someone wants to make it up with you.

VALERIE: Who? Erich?

OSKAR: No.

VALERIE: Then who?

OSKAR: Him.

(*VALERIE approaches the butcher's and sees ALFRED.
ALFRED bows. Pause.*)

VALERIE: Oh.

(*The music has stopped again.*)

ALFRED: You've no idea the inner struggles this has cost me,
coming to eat humble pie like this. But I'm not ashamed to
do it any more, because I know I treated you badly.

VALERIE: Me?

ALFRED: Yes.

VALERIE: When was that, then?

(*ALFRED is puzzled.*)

You've never done me any harm.

(*ALFRED is even more puzzled. He smiles, embarrassed.*)

ALFRED: Well, after all, I did leave you…

VALERIE: You left me? I left you! Anyway, there was no
harm in that, it was a very good thing, and don't you forget
it, you vain monkey!

ALFRED: We parted good friends, though, didn't we?

VALERIE: We parted, didn't we, and that was that! I'm not
going to have anything more to do with a complete swine!

(*Silence.*)

ALFRED: What do you mean, a complete swine? You just
said I didn't do you any harm.

VALERIE: I'm not talking about me! I'm talking about
Marianne! And your baby!

(*Silence.*)

ALFRED: Marianne always said I must be a hypnotist…
(*He shouts at her.*) Is it my fault I have such a powerful effect
on women?

VALERIE: Don't you shout at me!

OSKAR: In my opinion, I mean, relatively speaking, Alfred
was rather good to Marianne.

VALERIE: You men, always helping each other out! I have
my share of female solidarity as well, you know.
(*To ALFRED.*) I'd like to see you cut down to size,
really cut down to size.
(*Silence.*)

ALFRED: I've been routed. You don't have to tell me twice
I'm a bad person, I know it, and the reason is, when it really
comes down to it, I'm weak. I've always needed someone
to look after, I have to have it, otherwise I'm lost. But I just
couldn't look after Marianne, that was just my bad luck…
I mean, if I'd still had some capital, I could have played the
horses, except she wouldn't
let me…

VALERIE: She wouldn't let you?

ALFRED: She thought it was immoral.

VALERIE: That was stupid of her, it's the only thing you're
any good at.

ALFRED: You see! And that's the only reason our relationship finally fell to pieces, different way of looking at things.
It was quite spontaneous.

VALERIE: You're a liar.
(*Silence.*)

ALFRED: Valerie. I sold skin cream, I sold fountain pens,
I sold Persian carpets… The whole thing was a disaster, and
now I'm really in a bloody awful situation. You used to be
so understanding about other people's complications…

VALERIE: (*Interrupting him.*) How was France?

ALFRED: Much the same as here.

VALERIE: And how were the French girls?

ALFRED: Same as they all are. Ungrateful.

VALERIE: (*Smiles.*) You bugger. What would you do, if I was
to lend you fifty schillings?
(*Silence.*)

ALFRED: Fifty?

VALERIE: Yes.

ALFRED: Well, of course, I'd send it straight off to
Maisons-Laffitte, win or a place…

VALERIE: (*Interrupting him.*) And then what?

ALFRED: How do you mean?

VALERIE: What would you do with the winnings?
(*Silence.*)
ALFRED: (*Cunning smile.*) The money I'd be likely to win,
I'd hand over personally to my son tomorrow...
VALERIE: I'll believe that when I see it!
(*MARIANNE enters quickly and stops, frightened.*)
OSKAR: Marianne!
VALERIE: Well, well!
(*MARIANNE looks from one to the other and starts to
leave, quickly.*)
Wait! Don't go! It's time we cleared up this mess, it's
spring-cleaning time. It's time to make things up once and
for all!
(*Silence.*)
OSKAR: Marianne. I'm quite prepared to forgive you for
everything you've done to me, because loving someone
brings you more happiness than being loved. If you have
a shred of feeling left in you, you must know that in spite
of everything, I'd take you to the altar today, that is if you
were still free, what I mean is, the child...
(*Silence.*)
MARIANNE: What are you talking about?
OSKAR: (*Smiles.*) I'm sorry.
MARIANNE: What about?
OSKAR: The child...
(*Silence.*)
MARIANNE: Leave the baby out of it, will you? What's the
baby done to you? And don't look at me in that stupid way!
VALERIE: Marianne! This is supposed to be a reconciliation.
MARIANNE: (*Pointing at ALFRED.*) Not with him!
VALERIE: Him as well. All or nothing. After all, he's only a
human being!
ALFRED: Thanks very much.
MARIANNE: Yesterday you said he was a mean-minded
animal.
VALERIE: Yesterday was yesterday, and today's today,
and anyway you mind your own business.
ALFRED: He who loves change alone will be my friend.
OSKAR: (*To MARIANNE.*)

If you love not in your heart
Death and resurrection,
You can only be a part
Of the world's infection.

MARIANNE: (*Grins.*) My God, you're educated.

OSKAR: Got it off a calendar.

VALERIE: Calendar or no calendar, he's only a human being after all, with all the inborn failings and vices. You just didn't give him the kind of stability he needs.

MARIANNE: I did my best!

VALERIE: You're just too young!

(*Silence.*)

ALFRED: When it comes down to it, I was no angel either.

VALERIE: When it comes down to it, it's really no-one's fault, that kind of a liaison. When it really comes down to it, it's all a question of the stars, some aura attracting us to each other and all that.

MARIANNE: But they locked me up.

(*Silence.*)

They really humiliated me.

OSKAR: Well, you can't expect the police to wear kid gloves.

VALERIE: At least they were women officers, weren't they?

MARIANNE: Some of them.

VALERIE: Well, then!

(*Silence.*)

Marianne, dear. What you must do now, is just go quietly in there...

(*She points to the dolls' hospital.*)

MARIANNE: Why?

VALERIE: Just go...

MARIANNE: Alright, it's your responsibility.

VALERIE: My responsibility.

(*Silence. MARIANNE turns slowly towards the dolls' hospital, puts her hand on the door-knob, then turns back to VALERIE, ALFRED and OSKAR.*)

MARIANNE: I just want to say one thing. When it really comes down to it, I don't give a shit. What I'm doing, I'm doing for Leopold, because none of this is his fault... (*She opens the door, and the peal of bells rings out, as if nothing had happened.*)

Scene 4

Out in the Wachau

Alfred's GRANDMOTHER is sitting in the sun and his MOTHER is peeling potatoes. And the pram is nowhere to be seen.

GRANDMOTHER: Frieda! Have you written the letter?

MOTHER: No.

GRANDMOTHER: Do you want me to write it?
(*Silence.*)
Since Alfred hasn't given us his address, we've got to write to her…

MOTHER: I'll do it, I'll do it. They'll blame us for not being more careful…

GRANDMOTHER: Us? You! You, you mean.

MOTHER: It wasn't my fault.

GRANDMOTHER: I suppose it was my idea, taking the baby? Well, it wasn't, it was your idea, because you wanted a sweet little thing in the house, that's what you said.
I was always against it. That kind of thing, it's nothing but trouble.

MOTHER: Alright. It's my fault as usual. Alright. And I suppose it was my fault little Leopold caught cold as well and went to Heaven? My God, it's all so terrible!
(*Silence.*)

GRANDMOTHER: Maybe it's not as terrible as all that.
I'm thinking about your Fräulein Marianne. You know what they are, those girls. Perhaps she'll be quite pleased to be rid of it…

MOTHER: Mama! Are you mad?

GRANDMOTHER: What are you talking about, you stupid cow?

MOTHER: What are you talking about, you monster? She is a mother, after all, just the same as you!

GRANDMOTHER: (*Shrieking.*) Don't you compare me with her! My child was born in wedlock, or perhaps you think you're a bastard? When there's no blessing from above, it always ends badly and so it should! Otherwise where would we be? Now it's time that letter was written, and if you're too scared to do it, I'll dictate it to you. (*She gets up.*) Sit down here. There's pencil and paper there. I've got it all ready.

MOTHER: Monster...

GRANDMOTHER: Shut up! Sit down! Write! Be thankful I'm helping you!

(*The MOTHER sits down. The GRANDMOTHER walks up and down, hunched up, and dictates.*)

Dear Fräulein. That's right, Fräulein! I'm afraid we have to inform you of a very sad piece of news for you. In his inscrutable wisdom, Almighty God has decreed, that you, dear Fräulein, no longer have a child. It was only a little cold, but the child passed away very quickly. Full stop. But you must be of good cheer, because Almighty God loves innocent children. Full stop. New paragraph.

(*MARIANNE enters, with the ZAUBERKÖNIG, VALERIE, OSKAR and ALFRED. She has hurried on a little ahead of them.*)

MARIANNE: Hello, Frau Zentner. Nice to see you, Grandmama! I know I haven't been here for some time, but I'm very pleased to see you again. This is my father.

(*The ZAUBERKÖNIG bows.*)

MOTHER: (*Noticing ALFRED.*) Alfred!

MARIANNE: (*Suddenly uneasy.*) What's the matter...?

(*The GRANDMOTHER hands her the letter. She takes it mechanically and looks around timidly.*)

(*Frightened.*) Where is he...? Where is he...?

GRANDMOTHER: Read it, please. Just read it.

(*MARIANNE reads the letter.*)

ZAUBERKÖNIG: Well, where's little Leopold, then?

(*He is holding a toy in his hand, with bells attached to it. He jingles it.*)

Grandpa's here! It's grandpa!

(*MARIANNE drops the letter. Silence.*)

(*Suddenly anxious.*) Marianne! Is something the matter?

(*VALERIE has picked up the letter and read it.*)

VALERIE: (*Crying out.*) Mother of God! He's dead! Little Leopold's gone!

ALFRED: Dead?

VALERIE: Dead!

(*She sobs. ALFRED automatically puts his arms round her. The ZAUBERKÖNIG staggers. He drops the toy and buries his face in his hands. Silence. The GRANDMOTHER picks up the toy, curious, and jingles it. MARIANNE watches her; then suddenly throws herself silently at her and tries to kill her with the zither, which is lying on the table. OSKAR grabs her round the throat. MARIANNE chokes and drops the zither. Silence. The GRANDMOTHER picks up the zither.*)

GRANDMOTHER: (*Quietly.*) You bitch. You pig. You gaolbird. You'd like to kill me, would you? Would you?

MOTHER: (*Suddenly shouting at the GRANDMOTHER.*) You get back in the house, go on, hurry up!

(*The GRANDMOTHER comes up to the MOTHER slowly.*)

GRANDMOTHER: That'd just suit you, wouldn't it, if I were in my grave, that's what you've been wanting for ages, isn't it? But I'm not going yet awhile, I'm not going yet. See? (*She slaps the MOTHER's face.*) Well, those of you who want me to die, I hope you all rot!

(*She exits into the cottage with her zither. Silence.*)

MOTHER: (*Sobbing.*) You'll be sorry for that!

(*She follows her in. The ZAUBERKÖNIG slowly takes his hands away from his face.*)

ZAUBERKÖNIG: Another heart attack, another heart attack, dear God, no, no, no, give me a little more time, God. (*He crosses himself.*) Our Father, which art in Heaven... God is great, God is just...you are just, God, aren't you? Give me a little more time, just a little. You are just, you are just! (*He straightens his tie and exits slowly.*)

VALERIE: (*To ALFRED.*) How old was he, little Leopold?

ALFRED: Not very old.

VALERIE: My most sincere condolences.

ALFRED: Thank you. (*He takes some banknotes out of his trouser pocket.*) Look. I sent off to Maisons-Laffitte yesterday and won. And today I wanted to give my son eighty-four schillings...

VALERIE: We'll buy him a nice tombstone. A praying angel, something along those lines.

ALFRED: I'm very sad. I really am. I was just thinking, just now, without children, you're really nothing. There's no continuity, you just become extinct. What a shame!

(*He exits slowly with VALERIE.*)

MARIANNE: I once asked God what was to become of me. He didn't tell me, otherwise I wouldn't be here any more. He didn't tell me anything. He wanted it to be a surprise. Damn Him!

OSKAR: Marianne! Never quarrel with God!

MARIANNE: Damn Him! Damn Him!

(*She spits. Silence.*)

OSKAR: Marianne. God knows what He's doing, believe me!

MARIANNE: Where's my baby? Where are you? Where?

OSKAR: He's in Paradise.

MARIANNE: There's no need to torment me...

OSKAR: I'm not a sadist. I'm only trying to comfort you. Your whole life still lies ahead of you. This is just the beginning. The Lord giveth and the Lord taketh away.

MARIANNE: He's done nothing but take away from me, nothing.

OSKAR: God is love, Marianne. And whom the Lord loveth, He chasteneth...

MARIANNE: He's beaten me like a dog!

OSKAR: Well, if it has to be, it has to be.

(*Inside the cottage, the GRANDMOTHER starts playing Johann Strauss's 'Tales from the Vienna Woods' on her zither.*)

Marianne. I once told you I hoped you'd never have to go through what you made me suffer. And even now God has left you people who love you in spite of everything. And now everything's been put right like this... I once told you, Marianne, you wouldn't escape my love...

MARIANNE: I'm finished. I'm finished now...

OSKAR: Come along, then...

(*He supports her, kisses her on the mouth and slowly exits with her. And there's a humming and ringing in the air, as if some heavenly string orchestra were playing the 'Tales from the Vienna Woods' by Johann Strauss.*)

The End.

Songs

ACT ONE, Scene 3 (page 98)

Sei gepriesen, du lauschige Nacht...

Glory be to that heavenly night,
When two young hearts their troth did plight.
Next year the altar-rose espied
The couple kneeling side by side!
And Mr Stork soon left his nest
And flew to their home with a bundle blest.
Although sweet May once again disappeared,
When you're young at heart it blooms every year.

ACT TWO, Scene 4 (page 121)

Es kam einst gezogen ein Bursch ganz allein...

A happy young wanderer all by himself
Came sauntering along once as evening fell.
It was then he encountered a glance and a smile
That would live in his memory a very long while.
Her cheeks were so rosy, her eyes were so bright,
Her hair was so golden, her face a delight.
The girl he had seen there long haunted his brain
And often he sang to himself this refrain:

Way out there in Wachau
The Danube flows so blue,
In a cottage among the vines,
Her face at the window shines.
Her lips are red as blood,
Her kisses taste so good,
Her eyes are violet blue,
The girl out in the Wachau.

ACT THREE, Scene 1 (page 132)

Da draussen in der Wachau...

Way out there in the Wachau
The Danube flows so blue,
In a cottage among the vines,
Her face at the window shines.
Her lips are red as blood,
Her kisses taste so good,
Her eyes are violet blue,
The girl out in the Wachau.

Es wird ein Wein sein...

There will be wines to drink
We won't be here to drink
And girls to smile upon
When we are dead and gone...

Drum gehn wir gern nach Nussdorf naus...

So off we go to old Nussdorf
To have some fun and games
And dance the night away
And hear the handsome yodellers sing
And in the wee small hours
Go staggering home, go staggering home!

ACT THREE, Scene 1 (page 133)

Ach, ich hab sie ja nur...

Oh, a kiss on the shoulder was all that I tried...
and the next thing was I felt the slap of her fan upon
my cheek.

ACT THREE, Scene 1 (page 136)

Mein Muatterl war a Weanerin...

My mother was from Vienna,
That's why I love it so,
With a love that I knew
From the first breath I drew
For this golden Vienna of mine!

Wien, Wien, nur du allein...

Vienna, you alone
Will be the city I call my own,
City of laughter and dreams come true
Vienna, I love you!

ACT THREE, Scene 1 (page 137)

Mir ist mei Alte gstorbn...

Oh, my old lady's dead
And I still feel the pain.
Such a kind-hearted soul
I'll never find again.
I can't help crying.
Don't think I'm lying
It makes me so upset
When I think of my old pet! Olé!

ACT THREE, Scene 1 (page 138)

Vindobona, du herrliche Stadt…

Vindobona, you beautiful city,
All your walks and parks are so pretty,
You will always live in our heart
And draw us to you when we're apart.
Where'er we wander, far or near,
We'll never forget our Vienna's here.
You'll always be old Austria's pearl,
The loveliest city in all the world!

Now Mizzi and her Jean
Go walking arm in arm,
We're not made out of stone,
We're young and full of go,
It's not jam every day,
But we're going to make hay,
Today we're going to Brady's
Or Maxim's for the ladies!
Let's crack another bottle of wine,
Hollodero!
And it won't be the last in line,
Hollodero!
And if it is, so what, says I
Hollodero!
We're going to sing it one more time, let's sing it one
more time!